W9-AJG-962

ELMORE LEONARD'S 10 RULES OF WRITING

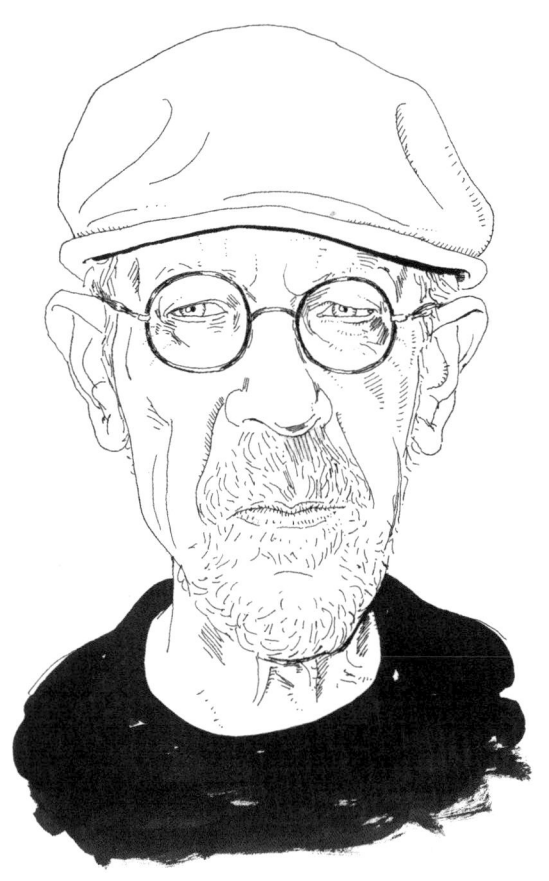

ELMORE LEONARD'S 10 RULES OF WRITING

Illustrations by
JOE CIARDIELLO

WILLIAM MORROW
An Imprint of HarperCollins*Publishers*

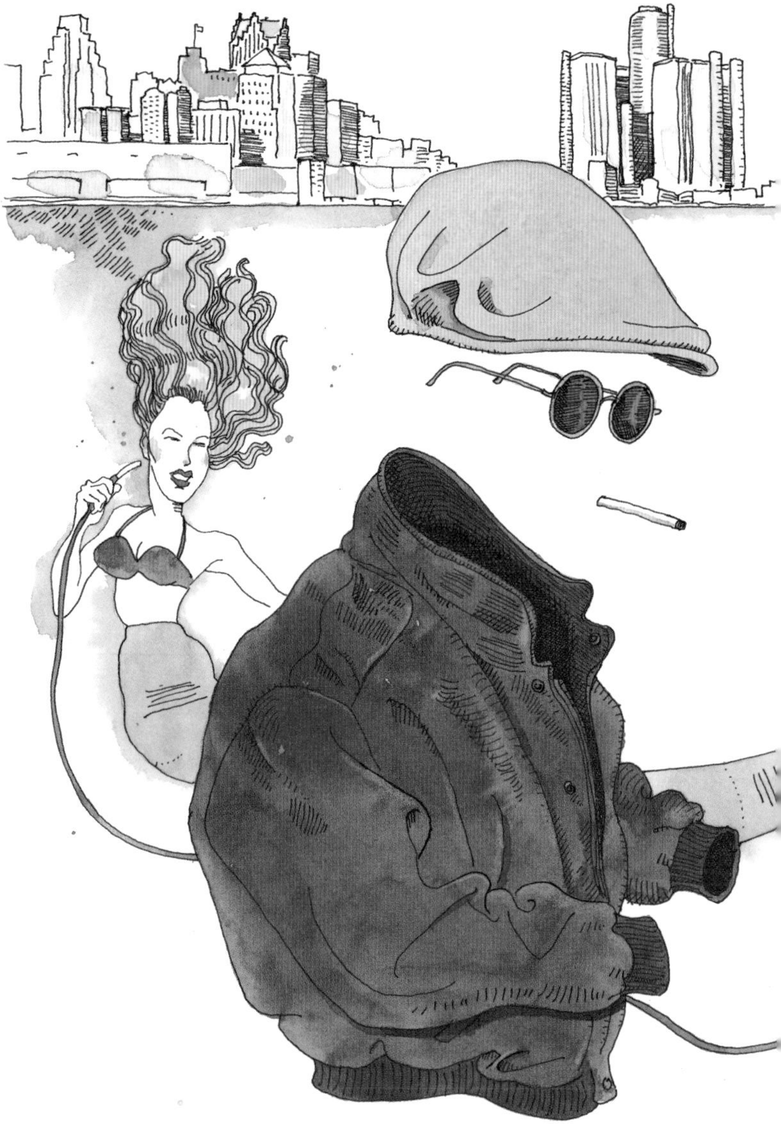

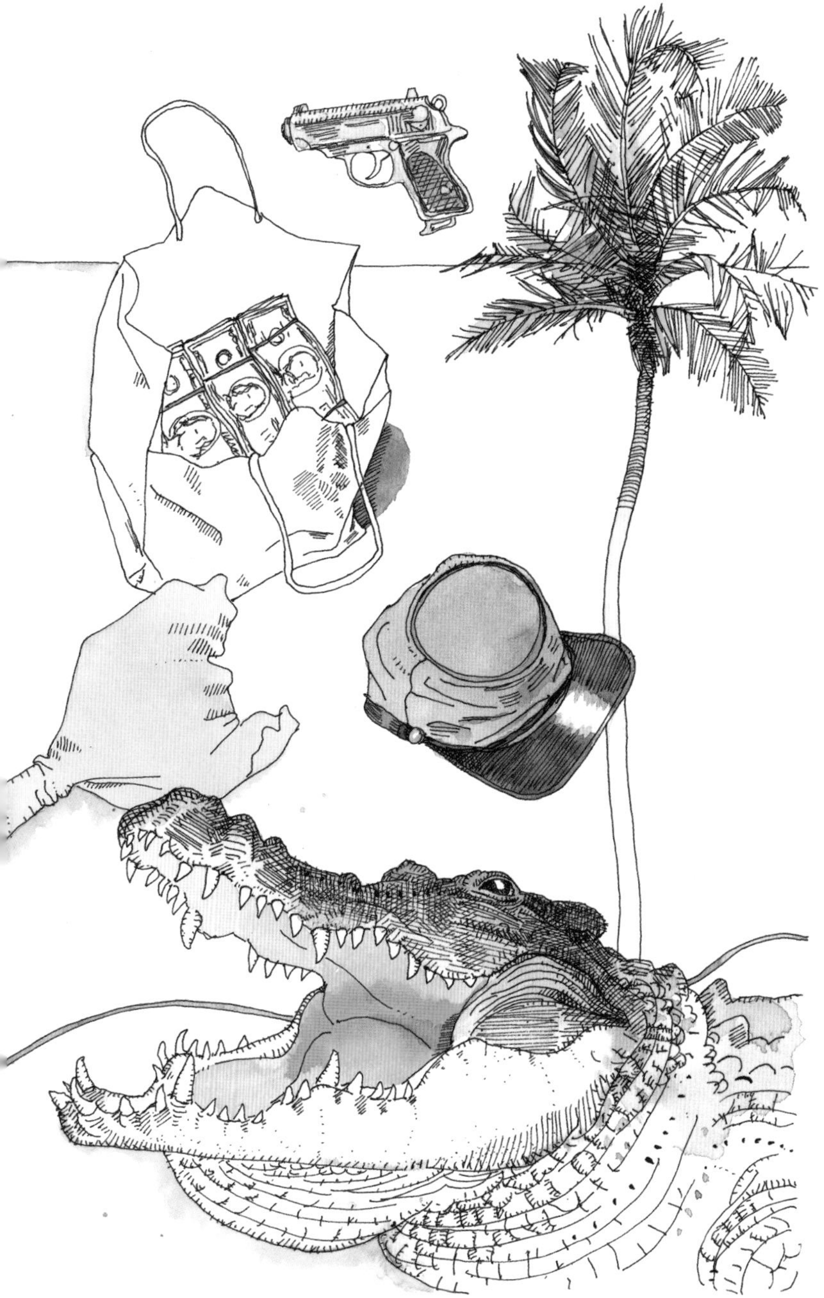

These are rules I've picked up along the way to help me remain invisible when I'm writing a book, to help me show rather than tell what's taking place in the story. If you have a facility for language and imagery and the sound of your voice pleases you, invisibility is not what you are after, and you can skip the rules. Still, you might look them over.

1.

NEVER OPEN A BOOK WITH WEATHER

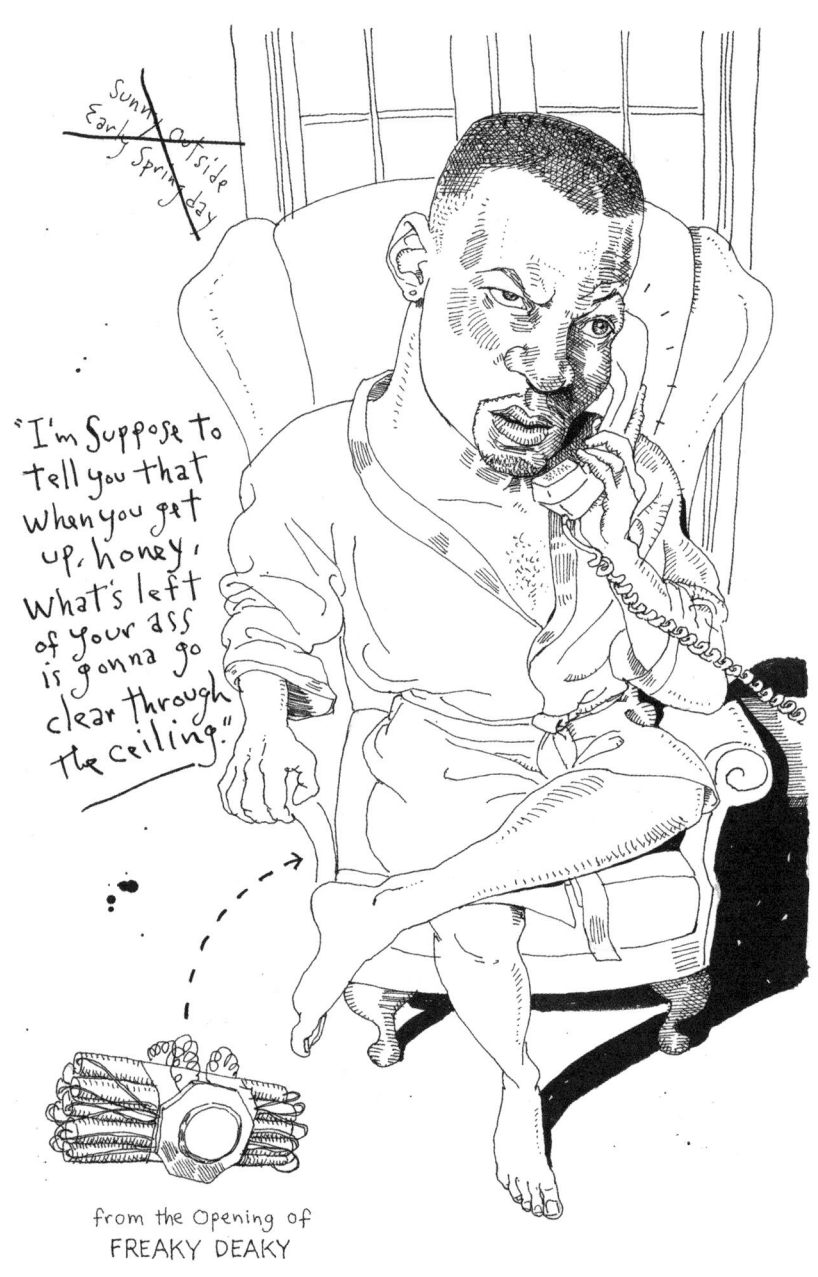

from the Opening of
FREAKY DEAKY

If it's only to create atmosphere, and not a character's reaction to the weather, you don't want to go on too long. The reader is apt to leaf ahead looking for people. There are exceptions. If you happen to be Barry Lopez, who has more ways than an Eskimo to describe ice and snow in his book *Arctic Dreams,* you can do all the weather reporting you want.

AVOID PROLOGUES

They can be annoying, especially a prologue following an introduction that comes after a foreword.

But these are ordinarily found in nonfiction. A prologue in a novel is backstory, and you can drop it in anywhere you want.

There is a prologue in John Steinbeck's *Sweet Thursday,* but it's okay because a character in the book makes the point of what my rules are all about. He says:

"I like a lot of talk in a book and I don't like to have nobody tell me what the guy that's talking looks like. I want to figure out what he looks like from the way he talks . . . figure out what the guy's thinking from what he says. I like some description but not too much of that."

The Steinbeck character goes on to say, "Sometimes I want a book to break loose with a bunch of hooptedoodle. . . . Spin up some pretty words maybe or sing a little song with language. That's nice. But I wish it was set aside so I don't have to read it. I don't want hooptedoodle to get mixed up with the story."

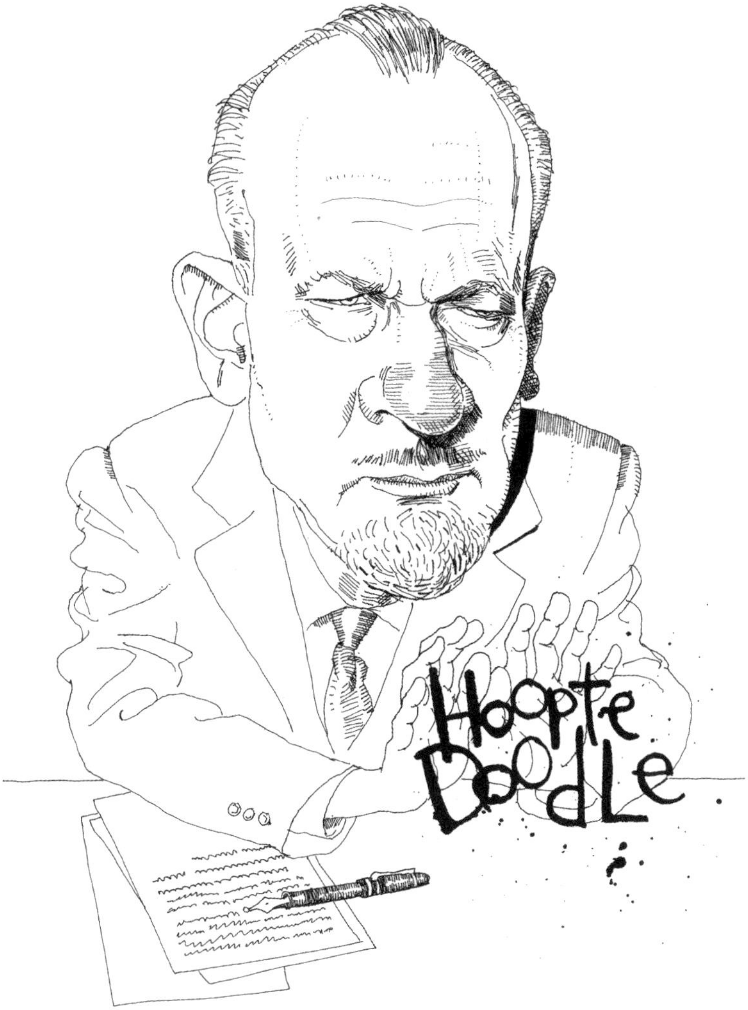
Hooptie
Doodle

3.

NEVER USE A VERB OTHER THAN "SAID" TO CARRY DIALOGUE

The line of dialogue belongs to the character; the verb is the writer sticking his nose in. But "said" is far less intrusive than "grumbled," "gasped," "cautioned," "lied." I once noticed Mary McCarthy ending a line of dialogue with "she asseverated," and had to stop reading and go to the dictionary.

as·sev·er·ate (ə-sev'ə-rāt'), v.t. [<L. <ad-, to + severus, severe], to state seriously or positively. —as·sev'er·a'tion, n.

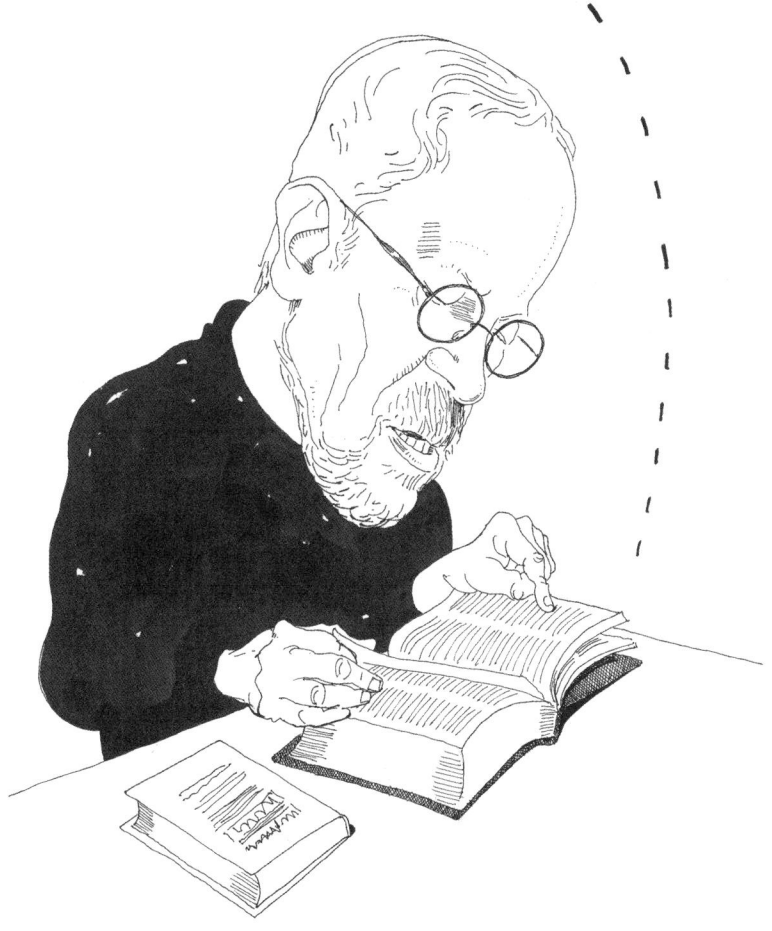

4.

NEVER USE AN ADVERB TO MODIFY THE VERB "SAID" . . .

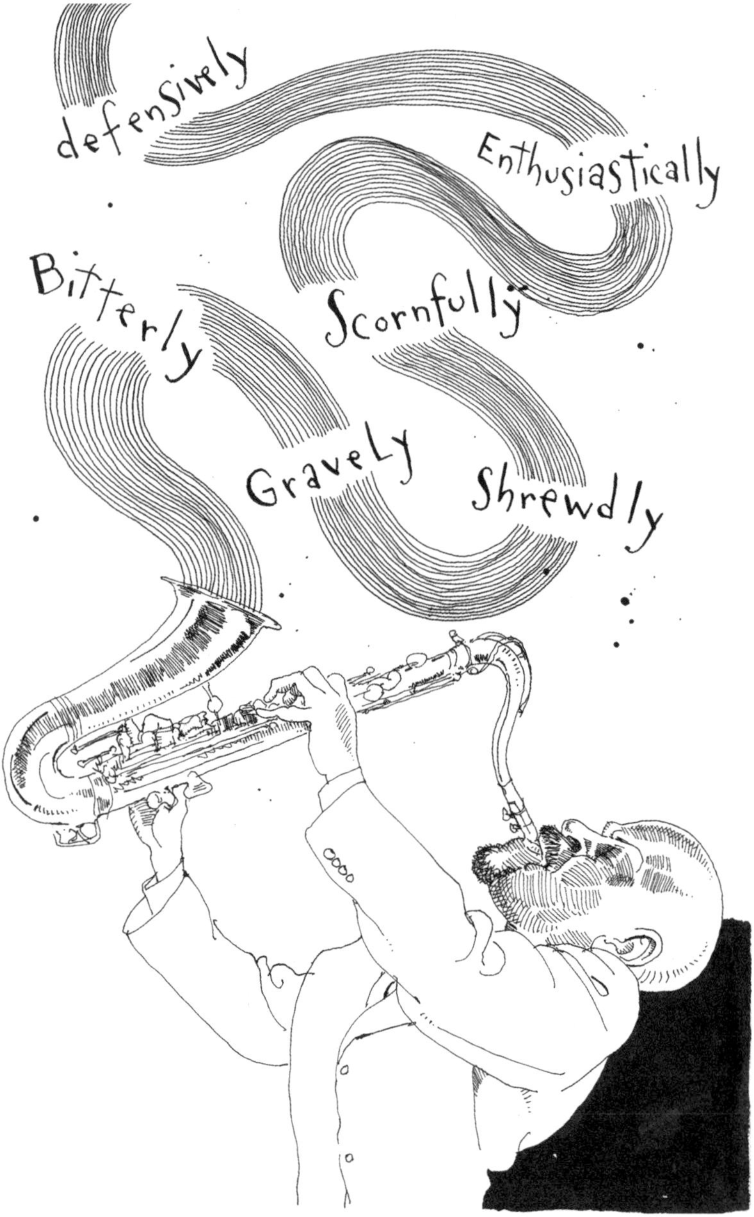
defensively
Enthusiastically
Bitterly
Scornfully
Gravely
Shrewdly

. . . he admonished gravely. To use an adverb this way (or almost any way) is a mortal sin. The writer is now exposing himself in earnest, using a word that distracts and can interrupt the rhythm of the exchange. I have a character in one of my books tell how she used to write historical romances "full of rape and adverbs."

5.

KEEP YOUR EXCLAMATION POINTS UNDER CONTROL

You are allowed no more than two or three per 100,000 words of prose. If you have the knack of playing with exclaimers the way Tom Wolfe does, you can throw them in by the handful.

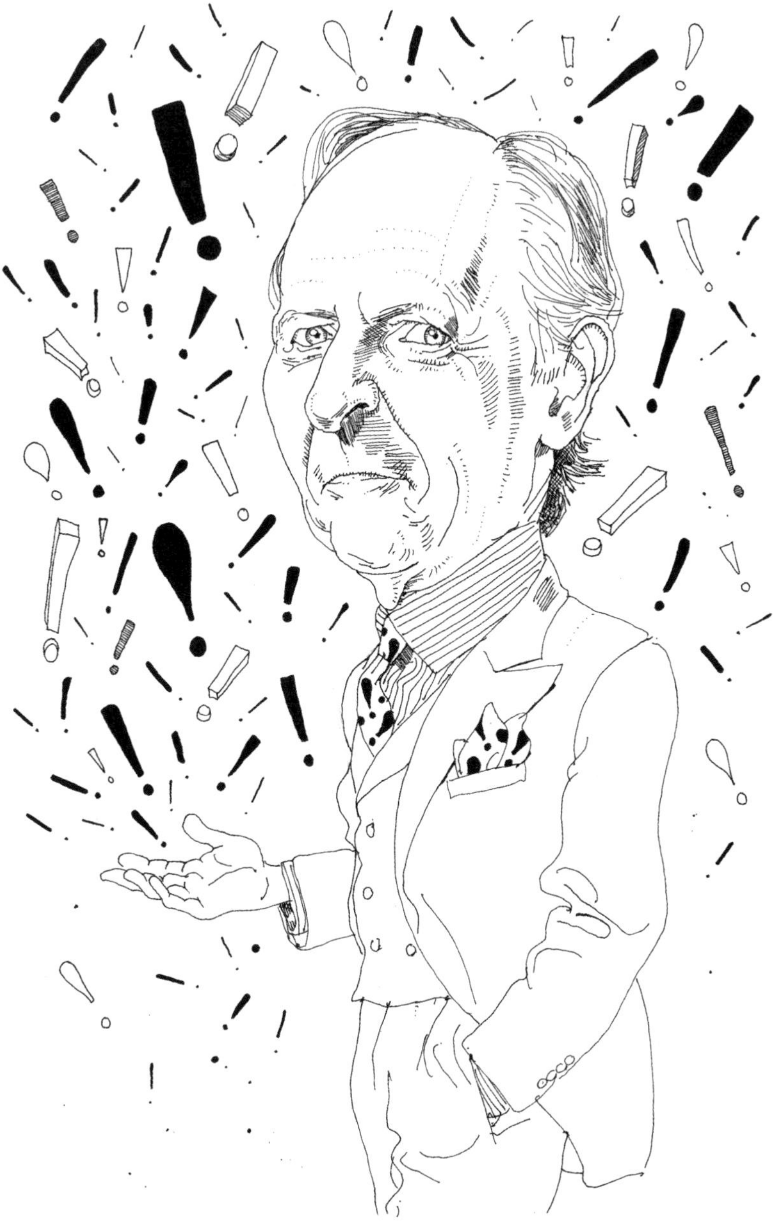

6.

NEVER USE THE WORDS "SUDDENLY" OR "ALL HELL BROKE LOOSE"

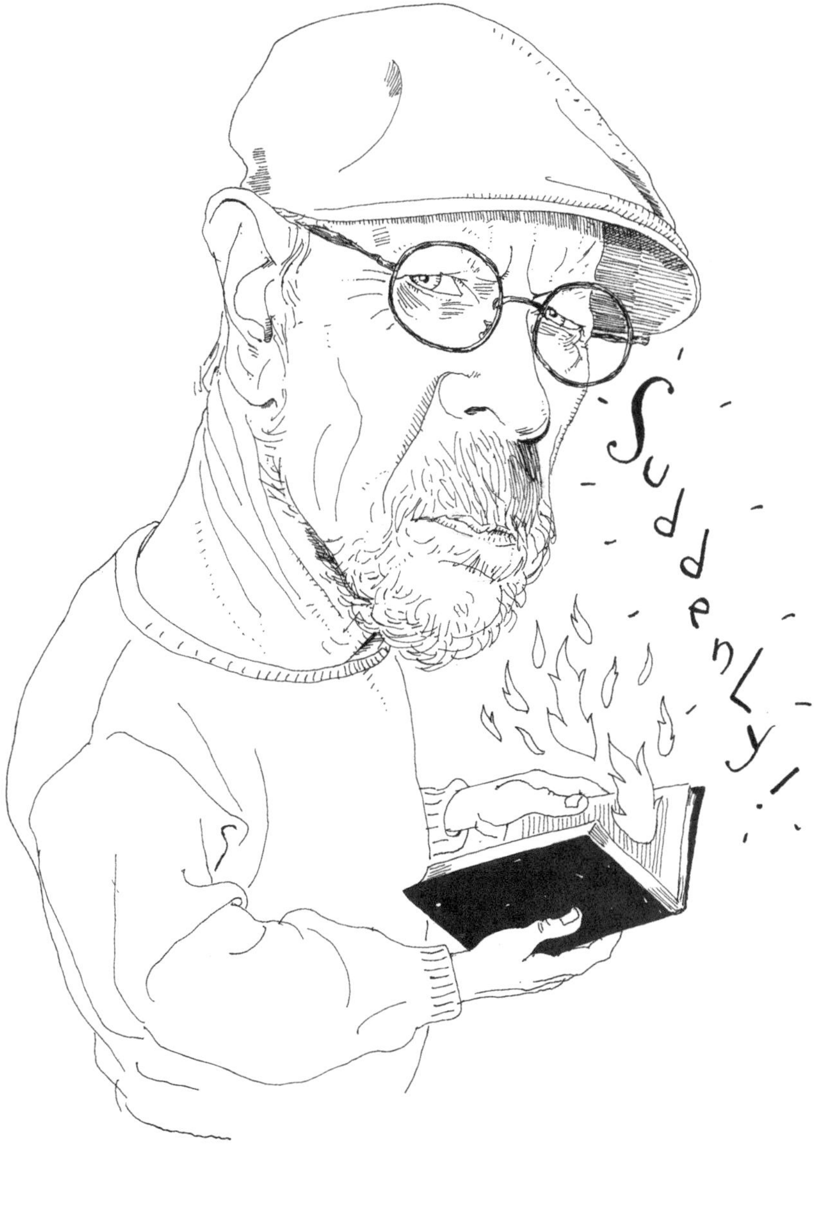
Suddenly!

This rule doesn't require an explanation. I have noticed that writers who use "suddenly" tend to exercise less control in the application of exclamation points.

7.

USE REGIONAL DIALECT, PATOIS, SPARINGLY

"Roland was working for the **EyetaLians** down in Miami when a woman shot him, said he broke into her house.

...It was her pulled the trigger, yeah, but was this dink set it up. He knew it was Roland in the house and told the woman it was somebody broke in. 'Cause he didn't have the nerve to do it hisself. Understand?"

ELVIN CROWE
from MAXIMUM BOB

Once you start spelling words in dialogue phonetically and loading the page with apostrophes, you won't be able to stop. Notice the way Annie Proulx captures the flavor of Wyoming voices in her book of short stories *Close Range*.

8.

AVOID DETAILED DESCRIPTIONS OF CHARACTERS

Which Steinbeck covered. In Ernest Hemingway's "Hills Like White Elephants," what do the "American and the girl with him" look like? "She had taken off her hat and put it on the table." That's the only reference to a physical description in the story, and yet we see the couple and know them by their tones of voice, with not one adverb in sight.

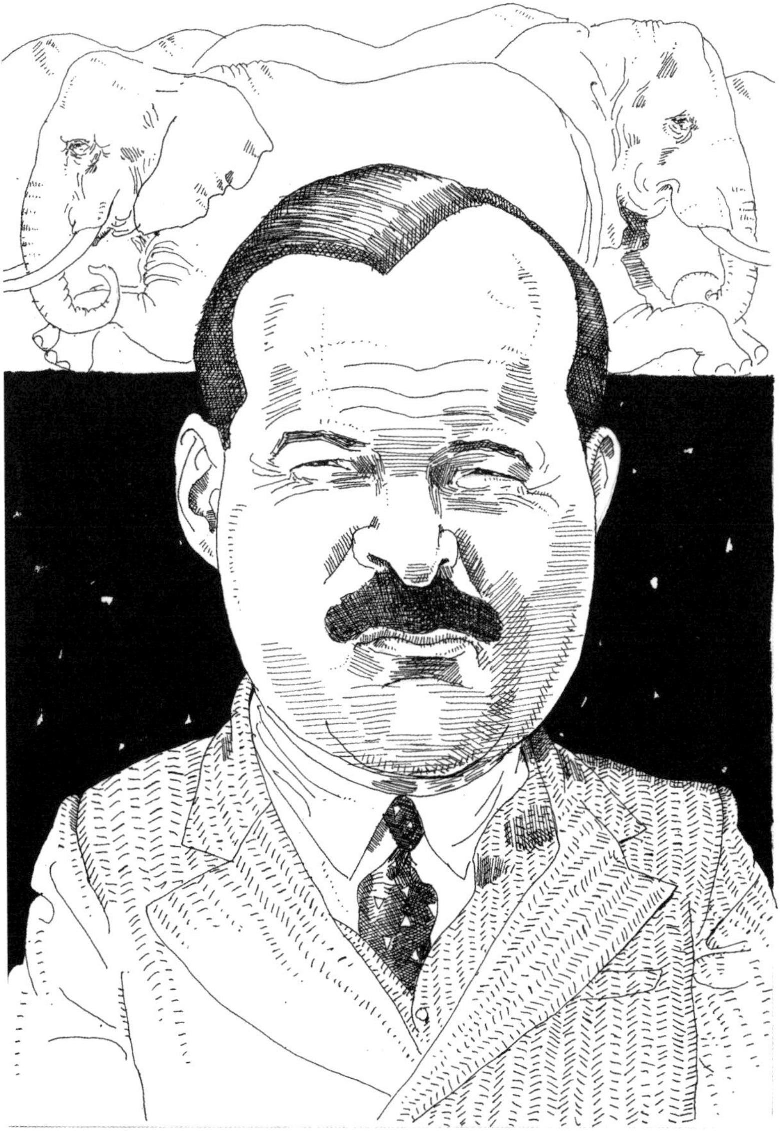

9.

DON'T GO INTO GREAT DETAIL DESCRIBING PLACES AND THINGS

Unless you're Margaret Atwood and can paint scenes with language or write landscapes in the style of Jim Harrison. But even if you're good at it, you don't want descriptions that bring the action, the flow of the story, to a standstill.

On the eastern horizon there's a grayish rosy, deadly glow: strange how the offshore towers stand out in that colour, a fir tree on it now with dark silhouette the deep against it risi of the pink and pale pond of the Lagoon. of the birds that nest out there and th ocean grinding against the reefs of rusted car parts and ju bricks and assorted rubble almost like holiday traffi

they pushed on further than usual to a beaver pond upstream on the creek. Berry climbed it now with still seems ti

The shrie
distant
ersat
bled
soun

waders
and hip
boots had
leaks that ex
ceeded the abil
ities of duct
It was
warmi
mornin
there
the ad
grea

out the b
of trout sh
could see from
her aerial
ition. B. D
waded in
his trous
becaus
both h

And finally:

10.

TRY TO LEAVE OUT THE PART THAT READERS TEND TO SKIP

A rule that came to mind in 1983, at lunch with Book-of-the-Month Club editors. Think of what you skip reading a novel: thick paragraphs of prose you can see have too many words in them.

What the writer is doing, he's writing, perpetrating hooptedoodle, perhaps taking another shot at the weather, or has gone into the character's head, and the reader either knows what the guy's thinking or doesn't care. I'll bet you don't skip dialogue.

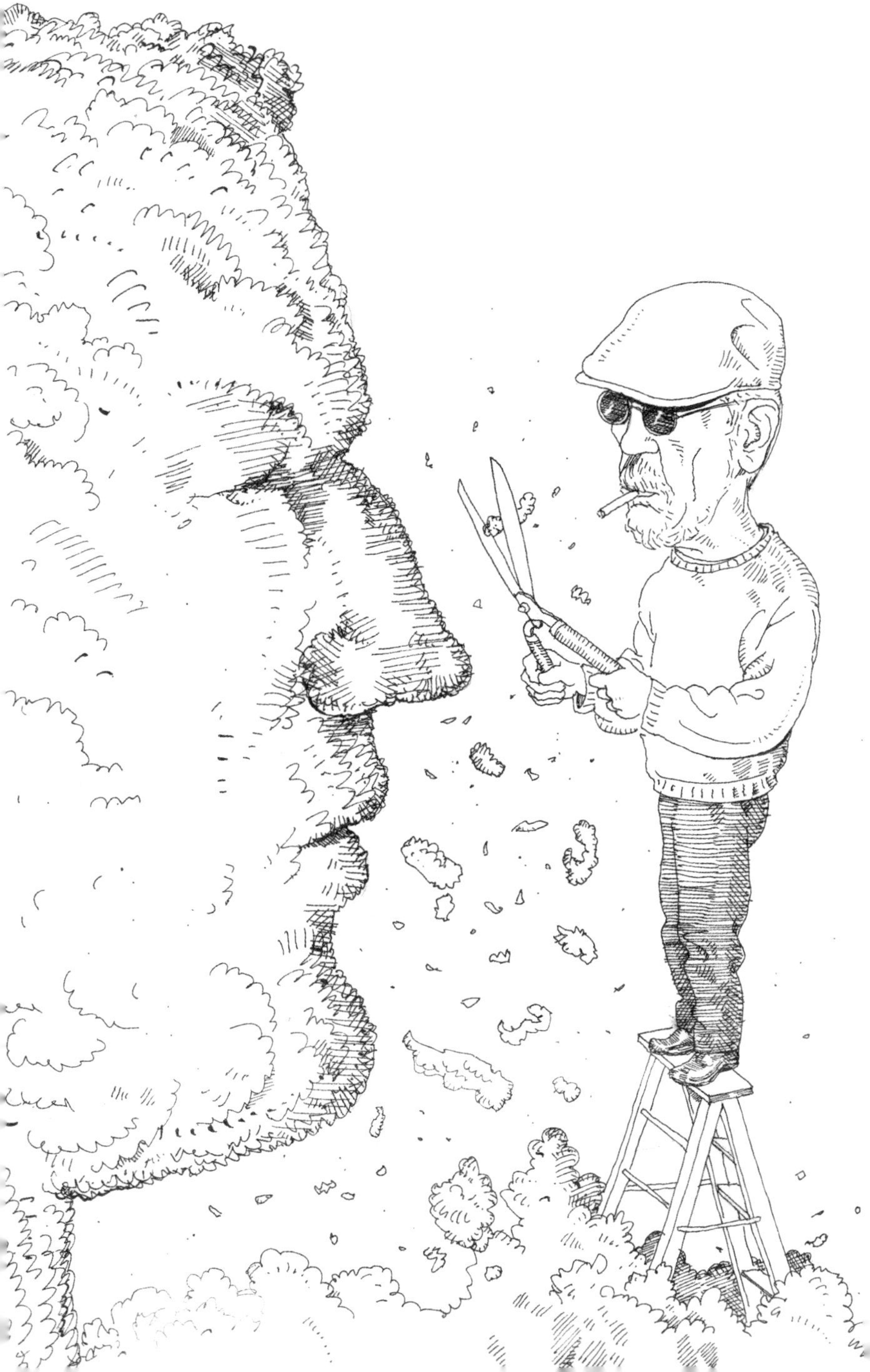

My most important rule is one that sums up the ten.

If it sounds like writing, I rewrite it.

Or, if proper usage gets in the way, it may have to go.

I can't allow what we learned in English composition to disrupt the sound and rhythm of the narrative.

It's my attempt to remain invisible, not distract the reader from the story with obvious writing.

(Joseph Conrad said something about words getting in the way of what you want to say.)

If I write in scenes and always from the point of view of a particular character—the one whose view best brings the scene to life—I'm able to concentrate on the voices of the characters telling you who they are and how they feel about what they see and what's going on, and I'm nowhere in sight.

What Steinbeck did in *Sweet Thursday* was title his chapters as an indication, though obscure, of what they cover. "Whom the Gods Love They Drive Nuts" is one, "Lousy Wednesday" another. The third chapter is titled "Hooptedoodle 1" and the thirty-eighth chapter "Hooptedoodle 2" as warnings to the reader, as if Steinbeck is saying: "Here's where you'll see me taking flights of fancy with my writing, and it won't get in the way of the story. Skip them if you want."

Sweet Thursday came out in 1954, when I was just beginning to be published, and I've never forgotten that prologue.

Did I read the hooptedoodle chapters?

Every word.

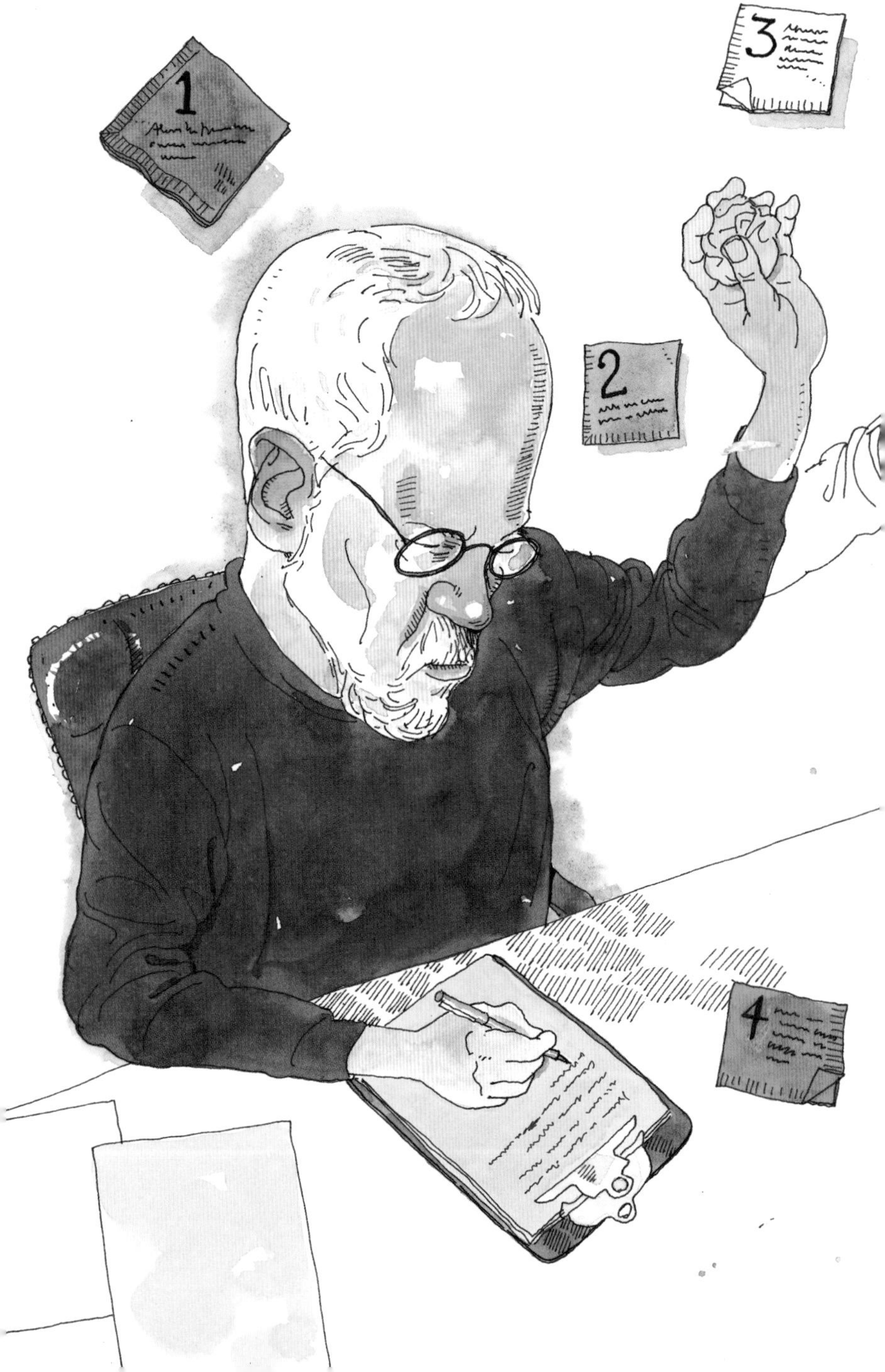
1
2
3
4

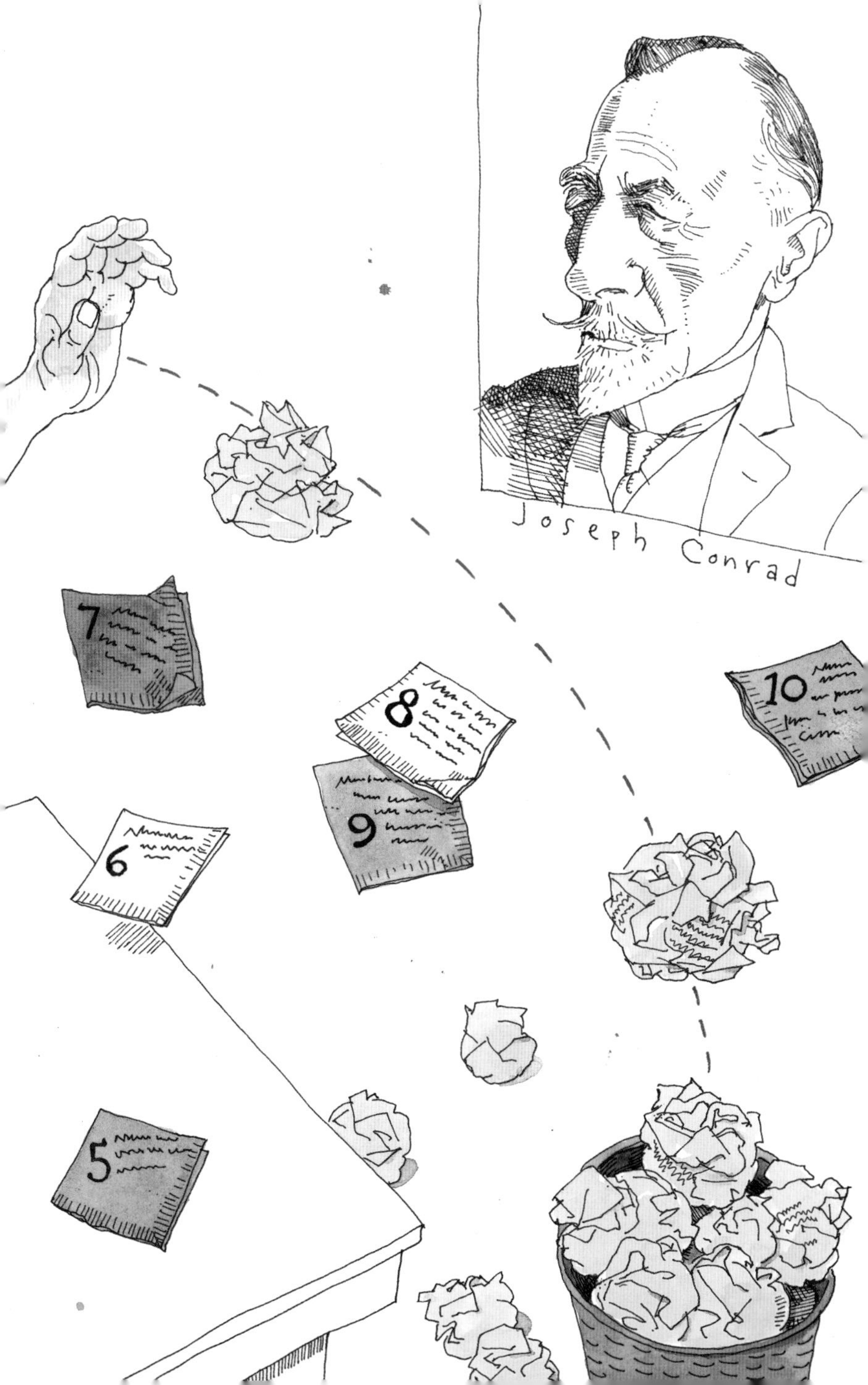
Joseph Conrad
7
8
10
9
6
5

Originally published in the *New York Times,* July 16, 2001, as "Easy on the Adverbs, Exclamation Points and Especially Hooptedoodle."

HarperCollins books may be purchased for educational, business, or sales promotional use. For information please write: Special Markets Department, HarperCollins Publishers, 10 East 53rd Street, New York, NY 10022.

FIRST EDITION

Library of Congress Cataloging-in-Publication Data has been applied for.

ISBN: 978-0-06-145146-1
ISBN-10: 0-06-145146-0

07 08 09 10 11 ID/TOPPAN 10 9 8 7 6 5 4 3 2 1

Possibilities and yearnings rose within his heart.

He'd known, since he was thirteen, what he wanted.

A home. A family.

Now he was thirty-five and staring at middle age, still single. And he was holding the sore ankle of a woman who was slowly, unwittingly, shifting into the emptiness of his life.

He pulled the wrapping snug and tacked the end of the bandage down. "That might not feel so good, but it will help," Luke said, standing up. "So. Supper. Guess I'll have to see what I can throw together."

"I should stay here," Janie sputtered. "I should supervise the kids."

"You should relax." Luke ignored her objections.

"But, Luke. The mess…" Janie's protest died as Luke shot her a warning look.

"I'll clean up," he said.

"Just make sure you do," she warned.

He saluted. "I'm a man of my word."

"Then you're a rare man indeed."

Books by Carolyne Aarsen

Love Inspired

Homecoming
Ever Faithful
A Bride at Last
The Cowboy's Bride
*A Family-Style Christmas
*A Mother at Heart
*A Family at Last
A Hero for Kelsey
Twin Blessings
Toward Home
Love Is Patient
A Heart's Refuge
Brought Together by Baby
A Silence in the Heart
Any Man of Mine
Yuletide Homecoming
Finally a Family
A Family for Luke

*Stealing Home

CAROLYNE AARSEN

and her husband, Richard, live on a small ranch in Northern Alberta, where they have raised four children and numerous foster children, and are still raising cattle. Carolyne crafts her stories in her office with a large west-facing window, through which she can watch the changing seasons while struggling to make her words obey.

A Family for Luke
Carolyne Aarsen

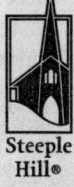

Steeple
Hill®

Published by Steeple Hill Books™

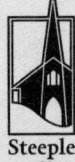

STEEPLE HILL BOOKS

Steeple Hill®

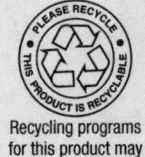

Recycling programs for this product may not exist in your area.

ISBN-13: 978-0-373-87512-2
ISBN-10:   0-373-87512-6

A FAMILY FOR LUKE

www.SteepleHill.com

Printed in U.S.A.

For if you forgive men when they sin against you,
your heavenly Father will also forgive you.
— *Matthew* 6:14

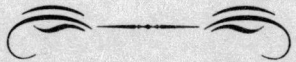

To my brothers and sisters.
Thanks for the memories.

Chapter One

"I don't want to talk to her." Luke moved his cell phone to his other ear as he stopped his truck in front of the derelict house. "Just transfer the money into her account like you always do."

Through the open window of his truck, he heard the sounds of saws screaming from inside the house, his most recent investment, hammers pounding and money being made.

"She really wants to see you." Uncle Chuck, his account manager, could be persistent when he thought Luke should do what he wanted. But Luke had lived around Uncle Chuck and his foster father, Al, long enough to pick up some of their quirks.

"You know, Uncle Chuck, when you see a dog and each time you try to pet it, it bites you, how quick are you going to be to pet it again?"

"But she says she's changed."

"Like all the other times she's changed. Sorry, Uncle Chuck. Not happening and that topic is now closed." Luke reached across the cab of the truck and pulled over a new cost estimate he had gotten from the foreman of the crew. "I'm gonna need more money in the building account. Push a few thousand in there, as well."

"Moving it as we speak. Are things going okay at the house?"

"I've had to move my trailer here until the job is done. So up to now, no, not going so good."

One of the construction workers sauntered down the ramp out the front door, his yellow hard hat askew on his head, a cigarette dangling from indifferent lips. He paused as he took a few more puffs before flicking the cigarette onto the lawn. He snagged a couple of two-by-fours, laid them on his shoulder and carted them back in. He could have easily brought in triple that.

"Efficiency is a problem. I'm sure I can get things going back on track if I'm physically here," Luke said, pulling out his metal clipboard. Then he jumped as a cold, wet nose was shoved in the back of his neck.

Cooper, his golden lab, heaved a canine sigh and laid his head on Luke's shoulder, expressing his frustration with the current level of inactivity. He'd been cooped up in the back of Luke's truck for the five-hour drive from Calgary north to the town of Riverbend.

At first Luke had toyed with the idea of putting Cooper in the holiday trailer he was pulling behind the truck, his temporary office and residence while he was supervising this house reno, but Cooper would get bored, and when he was bored he chewed. Anything. Pillows. Telephones. Cushions. Curtains. Any of the dozens of books Luke always took with him. If Cooper could get his mouth around it, he would chew it. So Cooper had spent the entire drive with his head hanging over the seat with expectant optimism.

"I really don't think you need to worry. You'll do okay," Chuck assured him, his voice turning crackly as the reception grew worse. "Have you thought of keeping this one for yourself? From the pictures you sent me, it has lots of potential."

Luke gave a short laugh as he got out of the truck to improve the reception. "This house is way too big for a bachelor. And the yard would take too much upkeep."

As he spoke, his gaze shifted to the yard next door. Grass so green it made his eyes hurt, a veranda holding chairs with fat, welcoming cushions.

And pots of flowers everywhere. Hanging from the sagging veranda roof, lined up on the crooked steps and at the end of a cracked and broken sidewalk.

The flowers seemed a valiant effort at hiding the broken-down condition of the house.

When he bought his current project a couple weeks ago, the Realtor had helpfully told him that the widow next door was young and had three children. As if this was all the information he needed to seal the deal.

"One of these days you're going to find someone," Gary had said in that avuncular way that could either set Luke's teeth on edge or make him smile.

Today he was feeling out of sorts. When he was done with this house it would be the fifth house he had rehabbed in the past three years. It would be the fifth time he put all his energy, imagination and personality into a house, only to turn around and let someone else settle into the home he had worked so hard to create. Truth be told, he was getting tired of the work. Getting tired of his life. Sure he wanted to settle down, and once upon a time, in a rosy and perfect past, he would have.

But Jocelyn kept putting off the wedding date, and after the fourth time, Luke gave her an ultimatum.

The next day he sold the house they had bought and since then, he had owned lots of houses but never had a home.

"You're my account manager, Chuck, not my personal adviser," Luke grumbled, shoving his hand through his hair.

He needed a haircut. It seemed he always needed a haircut. And a shave. Just too busy to keep up the appearances. No wonder he was still single.

"I'm also your uncle. And ever since Al died, I'm allowed to take over his father role."

Chuck's quick claim on Luke made him smile. From the day Luke had come to Al's home as a surly twelve-year-old foster child, Al's brother, Chuck, had insisted Luke call him Uncle.

"I don't need a father anymore, Chuck," Luke said.

"Everyone needs a father. I still miss my father. Especially now with Al gone."

"How are you doing?" Luke asked, leaning against the warm hood of the truck, his gaze alternating between his money pit and the house beside it.

Three kids and a widow.

"I'm okay. Sure, I miss my brother, but I'm more worried about you. You didn't stick around very long after the funeral."

Guilt settled around Luke like a dark cloud. "I know. I'm sorry. It's just…" his voice petered out.

"Okay. I won't push. But you make sure when you're done with that house up in the wilds of Northern Alberta that you come down to Victoria and see me and your Aunt Rose."

"I will."

"And as for Lillian?"

"Uncle Chuck, don't push. And don't tell her where I live."

The pause in the conversation told him this warning had come too late.

"I'm sorry. I thought I was helping."

"Maybe she'll just hit a bar and forget what you told her. But I gotta go. Take care, and I'll call you in a couple of days."

Luke said goodbye, then snapped his phone shut and slipped it in his pocket.

A whine from the truck shifted his attention from the past to the present. He should take Cooper for a walk. The poor dog had been patient the long drive up. Maybe he could put him in the backyard.

He walked across the overgrown, patchy lawn, the line of demarcation between his and the neighbor's lawn a stubby hedge leading to a rickety fence separating the backyards. A perfect before and after image, Luke thought. Green and lush on one side, and decidedly otherwise on his side.

The worn fence listed to one side.

The yard was in even worse shape than the house. Paint cans were piled in a tumbled heap against the fence. Discarded bicycle bodies lay rusted on the overgrown grass beside endless stacks of misshapen cardboard boxes. The only thing missing was a car jacked up on blocks.

He thought the crew might have done some cleaning up, but no.

Luke glanced from the decrepit yard to the house. Gary had been right about the place's promise. The huge yard, the corner lot, the older house with its gabled dormers and bay windows, all created potential curb appeal.

It would make a great family home, Luke thought with a touch of wistfulness. All it needed was a major cash input and, well, a family.

The money Luke had. The soft drink franchise he and his foster father, Al, had run had done okay. And when Al died, Luke sold the business. He'd never had a heart for it, so he turned his attention to real estate. He had enough money to move quickly on old houses, hire the right crews and wait until the market grew favorable to sell them.

Money wasn't the problem.

But family? Somehow, money couldn't solve that particular problem.

Luke turned back to the yard, imagining away the junk, the overgrown grass and picturing children in the yard, a wife sitting in a chair. His dog snoozing in the sun.

The perfect suburban family.

The family he thought he'd have a good start on by now.

A flash of color from the other yard distracted him from his internal grumbling. A little girl was tossing a stuffed bear into the air, her brown curls bouncing and bobbling as she picked it up and threw it again. A little boy sat on the steps overlooking the yard, bent over a book.

"C'mon, Todd," the little girl said. "Come and play with me and Berry Bear."

"I want to finish this chapter before Mom comes," Todd replied.

A memory teased Luke's consciousness as he watched the boy. Himself at exactly the same age doing exactly the same thing. Only no younger sister nagged at him to come and play. No mother was expected home any minute. He read because in the stories he immersed himself in, things always turned out okay by the end. Reading was his escape from the empty mobile home and the ever-present fear that his mom might not come home that night.

Go play with your sister, Luke silently urged the boy. You don't know how lucky you are.

Cooper's bark broke into his memories. Luke pushed himself away from the fence as Cooper barked again. He had to take the dog out of the truck.

As he turned, a woman pulled up behind his trailer and got out of the car.

The widow, he presumed.

She was younger than he had imagined. Slimmer. Dark hair pulled back under a bandanna, dark eyebrows that winged upward enhancing her eyes. She had a droop to her shoulders, but then she stopped at the end of the sidewalk and a gentle smile eased across her lips. She bent over the flowerpots, picked a wilted blossom out of it and her eyes seemed to brighten.

Luke was still watching her as he walked to his truck and opened the door for his dog.

Bad idea.

Seeing his moment of freedom, Cooper bolted past him, almost knocking him over.

Luke caught himself on the edge of the door, regaining his balance and watched with the horror of inevitability as his Cooper streaked down the sidewalk, all legs and flapping ears and lolling tongue.

"Cooper. Come back here now," he yelled, as if what he said penetrated the gray matter that was his dog's brain.

Cooper was out, and he was in a new place full of new smells and new things to see. His master was, for the moment, invisible.

"Cooper. Heel," Luke shouted, charging around the front of the truck.

Cooper stopped, and for a brief moment Luke thought all those dog obedience classes might have sunk in.

But the woman bending over the flowerpots had caught his attention. A potential playmate. And with one burst of exuberant energy, Cooper jumped on top of her just as he always did to Luke.

Only, this woman wasn't as big as Luke and she went down like a rock, taking the flowerpots with her.

The woman managed to push Cooper off her and scrambled to her feet just as Luke ran up. Cooper cavorted on the lawn in front of her, ready to play.

"Sit, you dumb mongrel," she snapped.

Cooper tilted his head, as if studying her.

"I said *sit*." She sounded really ticked now.

And to Luke's surprise, Cooper did. Right on the flowers that had spilled out of the pot, effectively squashing them.

"I don't believe this," she said, turning her startlingly blue eyes to him as he grabbed Cooper's collar. "This is like a nightmare."

Even though her mouth was pulled tight with disapproval, she couldn't hide the fullness of her lips or the delicate tilt of her cheekbones. He couldn't rightly say she was cute when she was angry, but he wanted her to smile again like she was when she had walked up the sidewalk.

Of course, he wasn't going to be the recipient of that happy occasion anytime soon, judging from the depth of her frown or the way her hands were clenched into tight fists.

"Sorry about that," Luke said, trying to sound apologetic without sounding obsequious.

"Could you please get your dog to get off my flowers?"

"Of course." He didn't apologize this time. That was getting old, and more apologies wouldn't change the destruction his dog had created. "I own the house next door," he said, trying to make conversation to bridge the awkwardness between them. "My name is Luke. Luke Harris."

"Janie Corbett," she said in a clipped voice, still glaring at Cooper, who was staring at her.

"I'll pay for whatever damage he's done."

"That's not necessary," Janie Corbett said. "And besides, these plants can't be replaced. They're very unusual."

"How unusual can flowers be?" Luke couldn't understand what she was talking about. Flowers were flowers, right? You buy some more, stick them in the pots and you're done.

"I started them myself from seed," she said bending over to salvage what she could from the mess Cooper had made. "And your dumb dog just ruined five months of work. Five months I can't reproduce."

Was that a hitch in her voice? Was she really that upset over a few lousy flowers?

Then the door to the house slammed open and the little girl with the brown curly hair bounced onto the deck, clutching her bear.

"Mommy. You're home," she called.

Distracted by this new person, Cooper leaped to his feet, barking and tugging on the collar.

"Luke, hang on to that dog," Janie cried out.

"Mommy. The dog."

Autumn's frightened voice caught Janie's attention and, it seemed, that ludicrous dog's. He barked again and took a step away from his owner, his focus on her daughter standing on the porch.

"Hold on to him," she shouted at Luke. It couldn't happen again. Please not again.

"Mommy." Autumn's voice grew panicky as the dog responded to her cry with unrestrained gusto.

Janie watched the creature pull free then rush toward Autumn, who had dropped her bear and now stood frozen on the porch.

"Cooper. Down. Now," Luke yelled in a feeble last-ditch effort.

Autumn's hands were pressed against her eyes, as if bracing herself for what might happen. Again.

But the dog came to a halt, then dropped to a squat on the sidewalk below Autumn, head cocked to one side.

"Luke, if that dog hurts her…" Janie couldn't finish the sentence; her voice was trembling too hard.

"I think he's okay," Luke said, edging closer to him.

The terror circling Janie's heart with an iron band eased as Luke reached for the dog's collar. Then the front door opened, and Todd stood in the doorway. Thankfully, both Todd and her elder daughter Suzie had been gone that horrible day. They didn't have the same reactions to dogs that Autumn did.

"Hey. Neat dog," he said, grinning.

Cooper, suddenly distracted, charged up the steps, past Autumn and through the open door behind him.

Janie ran to Autumn's side. She knelt, touching her daughter's face looking for any sign of trauma. "Are you okay, honey?"

Autumn looked puzzled, as if surprised that nothing had happened this time. The trembling smile she gave her mother made Janie's knees weak with relief.

Janie scooped up her daughter into her arms and gave her a quick hug just as she heard her own mother's outraged voice from inside the house.

"*What* is going on in the bathroom?"

Janie heard a bark, then the sound of water being lapped up. Oh, my goodness, was that dog drinking out of the toilet?

"I'm sorry, Mom," Todd said as Janie held Autumn close. "I didn't think he would come in the house."

"That's okay, Todd." Janie needed to go inside and see what that dog was doing, but she couldn't leave Autumn outside. She caught her son by the hand and led him and Autumn to the porch swing. "Sit here and don't move."

"But I want to see the dog," Todd complained.

"You need to stay with Autumn. You know why she's afraid of dogs."

"I'm not afraid of dogs." Todd offered, putting his arm around his sister.

"What's going on?" Now her own mother was outside and the dog was barking inside. "How did that creature get into the house? You must get him out. Immediately." Then Tilly saw Autumn and swooped down. "Is she okay, Janie? Did that dog hurt her? How could you let this happen?"

Janie felt like clapping her hands over her ears and retreating somewhere. Anywhere but here.

She'd spent most of the afternoon making coffee for her customers and trying to balance the books of her coffee shop. Though the customers kept coming, there was still a negative sign in front of the final balance in the checkbook, an irony not lost on her.

She and her oldest daughter, Suzie, had had a fight this morning over the skimpy skirt Suzie insisted on wearing, which made her look closer to twenty than fourteen, and Autumn had thrown up all over her precious bear. The phone call from Todd's teacher expressing her concern over Todd's constant reading during lunchtime was another nice touch.

And then, on the way home, her car started making funny noises that weren't the least bit humorous to her.

As a result, the ache perched behind her eyes all day had spread to her entire head, making it pound and throb.

When she'd turned onto her street, she had been so tempted to keep going past the house and down the road to the highway. Away from responsibilities and the constant demands on a single mother trying to juggle family and work.

But that was her ex-husband's trick. Not hers. Not responsible Janie Corbett. And as a result, she had been attacked by a crazed dog that was now loose in her house. Her new neighbor was yelling up the stairs, and her mother was staring at her as if this entire chaotic mess was her fault.

Somewhere there had to be a lesson in all of this.

"So how did that dog get in the house?" Tilly continued, pressing Janie for an answer.

"I let the dog in, Grandma," Todd said quietly. "He was looking at Autumn."

Tilly pulled back, her hands fluttering over her grand-daughter's face. "Honey, are you okay? Is she okay?"

Though the edge of anxiety in Tilly's voice echoed her previous fear, Janie resented the way her mother's tone elevated the concern in her daughter's face.

"Autumn's fine, Mom. Please, don't fuss."

The look her mother gave her held a volume of unspoken fears and concerns laced with reprimand.

"Don't fuss? Don't fuss? This precious child was bitten by Owen's dog only a few years ago. How could you forget that?"

Janie felt suitably chastened and, at the same time, guilty. It had been Tilly whom Janie called after she took Autumn to the emergency room and Tilly who had shown up to give her the support she should have been getting from her husband, Owen.

Even when Janie brought Autumn home, shivering with fear from being taken to the E.R., Owen was still not answering his phone. Janie had had to call the SPCA herself to come and get the dog.

"Cooper, come here," she heard from inside the house.

"Janie, shouldn't you go in and help him?" her mother asked.

"And do what?" Why did her mother think she could do anything with that out-of-control dog?

Tilly ignored Janie's outburst as she held Autumn close. "And you, baby, how are you? That dog must have scared you half to death." Tilly shot Janie an annoyed look.

With her headache subsiding, Janie trudged inside to see what she could do.

Luke stood at the foot of the stairs, one foot on the lower steps, his knee showing through a hole in his pants and the sleeves of his faded shirt rolled over his forearms.

His long, brown hair, curling over his collar and his unshaven cheeks would have looked slovenly on some men, but the even planes of his face created an appeal not lost on Janie.

And when he gave her a sidelong glance, she felt the vague beginnings of feelings so long dormant she hadn't thought they even existed.

"Sorry. Still don't have the dog," he said, an apologetic note in his voice.

"What is taking so long?"

"I didn't think you'd appreciate a complete stranger tromping through your house. Bad enough that my dog is."

"Well, go get him if you need to," she snapped, her headache, her recent scare with her daughter and the disturbing way he was looking at her giving her voice a sharp edge. Autumn was fine, but she didn't want to take any chances. She wanted the dog and this unsettling man out of her house.

She heard a thumping sound from upstairs and then, thankfully, a few seconds later Suzie came down, holding a panting dog by the collar.

And Suzie was doing something she hadn't done for months.

Her daughter was laughing. And not just a soft chuckle. No, this was a full-bodied laugh that made her eyes sparkle, her face light up and made Janie forget the skimpy skirt and tight

T-shirt she was wearing that had caused such a huge battle only a few hours ago.

"Here. I'll take him." Luke met Suzie halfway up the stairs and took the squirming dog from her. He looked up at Janie. "And again, I'm so sorry."

Her kids were okay and, from what she could see, no serious damage had been done to the house. And Luke wasn't looking at her anymore. She just wanted to be alone.

"Just go. Please."

"Does he have that ridiculous beast under control?" Tilly called out from outside. "Should I call 911?"

Janie glanced down at the dog, now sitting with his head tipped quizzically to one side, water still dripping from his snout. He seemed harmless. The emphasis on *seemed*.

"It's under control, Mom," Janie called over her shoulder. She arched an eyebrow at Luke, as if making sure.

"I'm leaving now." Luke had a firm grip on the dog's collar, and Janie took a quick step back.

"He won't hurt you." Luke's eyes locked on to hers, and he tilted her a quick smile.

As their eyes held that twinge returned, but she ruthlessly quashed it. Single mom. Three kids. As if she had any space for even the faintest hint of flirtation.

"Just make sure you keep that dog away from my kids, okay?" she said, disliking the harsh tone that self-preservation had put into her voice.

Luke held her gaze, as if surprised at her anger. Well, he could stay surprised. She didn't need to explain anything more to him.

But in spite of herself, she watched as he made his way down the walk, his six-foot-something frame bent over the dog to control him.

"Oh, my. Look at the mess," Tilly said as they stepped back in the house. "This has got to be cleaned up immediately. And if you want to keep those flowers outside in good shape, they'll need to be dealt with, as well."

Janie would have preferred to deal with the flowers and ignore the mess in the house.

But her mother was already picking up the coatrack and clucking about the relatively minor mess.

"Cooper was hilarious." Todd plopped onto the couch, a grin splitting his face.

"When I came upstairs, he was on my bed." Suzie was still chuckling as she pushed a tossed pillow aside and sat on the floor.

"Was he jumping?" Autumn asked.

"No. Just standing there, his head tipped to one side, looking like he was laughing." Suzie's smile shone like sunshine on a cloudy day.

"That man had to drag him away," Todd said. "I think the dog wants to play with us."

"You should have seen him in the kitchen after he'd been drinking out of the toilet," Suzie continued. "He came running off the carpet and couldn't stop. He slid right into the cupboard, feet up in the air. It looked so...so..." Suzie couldn't continue, she was laughing so hard.

Janie's heart contracted at the sound of her children's laughter, at their smiles and sparkling eyes. How long had it been since they'd been this happy?

Since before Owen left, that's when. In spite of his many failings as a husband, he could, at times, have fun with the kids. Make them laugh. Do goofy things with them.

Things Janie never had time to do.

"But then I had to bring him downstairs." Suzie glanced at

Janie, and she saw her daughter's mirth subside. As if it was her fault the fun had ended.

"What did the dog do on the bed?" Janie asked, trying to maintain the moment.

"Nothing. He didn't do anything."

Her voice had taken on a defensive tone that usually set Janie's teeth on edge, but in this case, it cut her like a knife. Suzie had misunderstood Janie's question.

Suzie held out her hand to Autumn. "Let's go play upstairs."

Janie felt a palpable cooling of the atmosphere as Autumn and Todd walked with their sister up the stairs.

Messed up again, she thought.

And for a moment the loneliness of parenthood settled on her like a musty old cloak. Always the boss. Always the cop, judge and jury. Always the one to end the fun.

"I think I'll be going," her mother said, brushing her hands on a handkerchief. "You should check upstairs. I'm sure there's going to be dog hair everywhere." Tilly shuddered.

"Thanks for coming on such short notice."

"That's what mothers do when babysitters leave you hanging." Tilly's amber eyes took stock of her daughter. "You're sure you're okay?"

"Mother, you're making more of this than necessary."

"I'm a little worried about that dog being next door."

"The town has a leash law. If Luke doesn't keep him tied up, he'll have the cops to reckon with."

"Well, he better keep it under control. The fence between the two yards isn't that strong. He could easily cross it. And then who knows what will happen?"

Janie had her worries as well about the fence and the dog, but if her concerns were put in order, these would be at the bottom of page four.

For now, she had a family to keep going, a business to keep above water, a loan to renegotiate, a hot water tank that needed replacing, gutters that needed cleaning, a roof that needed to be reshingled, a wall that needed repairing…

And stop. Focus on the now.

"…and your father is going to be gone most of this month on some business, so if you need anything, I'll be glad to help," Tilly said.

"Sure. Thanks, Mom. I appreciate the help."

Tilly's smile softened. "I want you to know I'm praying for you. I know it's been a year and a half since Owen died, but I'm sure you still have your difficult moments."

And again Janie kept her reply vague. Her mother still didn't understand that Janie hadn't missed Owen since he walked out on her and the kids three years earlier.

Owen around had proved to be more dangerous than Owen gone. Owen gone didn't drain her bank account. Owen gone didn't make her feel as if she and the children were a huge impediment to his happiness. Owen gone was a relief, and his death had morphed her from abandoned woman to widow, an infinitely more respectable situation.

"I'm sure there are times you wish you had someone, though," Tilly continued, laying her hand on Janie's arm. "I keep praying that the Lord will bring someone into your life. Someone who can be a father to your children and a support to you."

And how was she supposed to answer that? The last thing Janie needed or wanted right now was a man in her life. A man would be one more obligation she didn't have time for. A man would mean opening her life, once again, to the possibility of brokenness and rejection.

No thanks. Her life was chaotic, but as long as she kept a

rein on her various obligations and duties, she was okay. One tiny change would disrupt the precarious hold she had on her life right now. Her children were her first priority, and there was no way she was going to push them aside for a man.

She gave her mother a smile to put her off the scent. "I'm so thankful for your and Dad's support."

"You know your father would give you more…"

"No, Mom, really. We're fine."

"Just a suggestion." Tilly pecked her on the cheek. "Now go and take care of those lovely children of yours."

And with that, Tilly left.

Janie closed the door behind her mother and then leaned against it, sighing. What on earth had gotten her mother going on that particular tack?

Surely not the man who had come barreling into her life just a few moments ago.

Her thoughts slipped back to the man who had stood in her house. The man who had given her a crooked smile that seemed to hint at interest.

Now's a good time to stop.

Then, as she pushed herself away, she caught the whiff of an unfamiliar scent that created the faintest sense of yearning.

Aftershave.

Chapter Two

"So this weekend's the only time we'll have to work on Sunday?" Bert heaved the sheet of drywall into the metal bin behind the fence of the yard.

"We need to get caught up."

Luke had to get this place done in three weeks. His partner, Gary, had arranged for an open house and had promised that it was going to be a big splash.

No pressure. No pressure at all.

"My missus wasn't too happy until I told her I was getting double time." Bert tugged on his gloves as he grinned. "Couldn't get me out of the house fast enough after that."

They walked back to the yard, and as Luke bent over to pick up the second chunk of drywall, he heard a voice.

"Where's your dog?"

Sounded like Todd, the kid from next door.

Luke looked around for the owner of the voice he barely heard above the din of the skill saw.

Bert poked Luke and pointed to the fence.

"Do you have him tied up?" Todd called out again.

Then Luke saw the hole where one of the vertical boards on his side had been broken off halfway up. The boy was kneeling, looking through the hole.

"I'll be back," he said to Bert, pointing to the rotting pieces of plywood lying on the overgrown grass. "Pile all of this up in that garbage bin and throw those bikes in there, too."

Then he walked over to the fence and crouched down, to get on eye level with Todd. All he could see of the boy was one hazel eye, a freckled nose and a space where two top teeth used to be. "I have him in my holiday trailer," Luke replied grinning at the boy.

"Doesn't he like to run around?" Todd asked.

"Oh, yes. When I'm finished cleaning up this yard, it will be safe for him to run around in."

"My mommy always said this fence was no good. We had to stay away from it when we had our other neighbors. They were bad."

From the condition of the house and the yard, Luke wasn't surprised at Todd's assessment. "What was the baddest thing about them?" he asked, curious as to what constituted bad in Todd's books.

"They drank beer. I don't think they were friends of Jesus," he said in a solemn voice.

Friends of Jesus. The quaint phrase made Luke smile. "So are you a friend of Jesus?"

Todd nodded, then smiled. "Are you?"

The question made a wave in the pool of guilt Luke had been mired in since his foster father's death. When the God of all creation, the God who was supposedly so benevolent and loving took Al, the only person who had been true family to Luke, he stopped going to church. He couldn't stand hearing the happy, joy, joy songs mocking his sadness. There didn't seem to be a place for pain and loss in church.

And today was Sunday, as the men working behind him had told him a number of times. As if he didn't know. He was pretty sure very few of them were friends of Jesus either. Sunday was for fishing, in their eyes.

"I think Jesus is a good person," he said instead, reluctant to drag this innocent young boy into his own particular battle with God.

"Can your dog come over to play with us again?" Todd asked, his question coming from left field.

Luke's knees were getting sore so he stood up and looked over the fence down to the boy below him, taking note of the flowerpots on the deck and the tidy yard. Not the best place for an overly playful lab. "I think it might be better if Cooper stayed in my yard."

"But I like to play with your dog." Todd's grin faded away as he stood up.

Luke was pretty sure Janie wouldn't let Todd come over to his yard, so he didn't make that offer.

"Hey, Todd, we have to get ready for church." Suzie, the oldest girl, came out onto the porch. Her clothing was more sedate for the occasion. "Mom says…" Her voice eased off when she saw Luke. With a grin, she came running over. "Is your dog with you?" she asked, grabbing the fence and leaning over it.

"Careful," Luke said. "I don't know how good this fence is."

"Not good at all, according to my mom." Suzie gave the boards a shake, and the whole fence listed farther.

"Mom said she was going to fix it," Todd said.

"Except she can't afford to," Suzie added.

Todd frowned. "Don't let Mom hear you say that. She'll get mad."

Then Suzie heaved a theatrical sigh. "Like she always does." But Suzie let go of the fence. "Where's Cooper?"

"Until I get this fence fixed, he has to stay in the trailer," Luke said.

"He can play in our yard," Suzie offered, a hopeful note in her voice.

Then the porch door opened again, and Janie appeared on the deck.

"Suzie. Todd. Come back to the house," she called out, her voice sharp as she carefully made her way down the wooden stairs of her porch.

Janie wore a narrow brown skirt and shirt, and her hair fell in soft waves on her shoulders. All dressed up for church, Luke figured, the faint niggle of guilt returning.

Her eyes flicked from Luke to Todd to Suzie as she scurried over to her children, as if to protect them from the bad, dangerous stranger.

"What are you two doing?"

Todd looked down as he drew away from the fence. "I was just trying to see Luke's dog," he mumbled, toeing the grass with his shoe. "I'm sorry, Mom."

Janie's stroked her son's hair. "That's okay, honey."

"We didn't do anything wrong," Suzie complained, her voice edging toward anger.

Janie's mouth compressed into a thin line, then she forced a smile as she glanced at Suzie. "Of course not. But we do need to go to church."

Suzie heaved a dramatic sigh, then flounced off, her skirt bouncing as she walked.

As Janie turned to him, Luke held up his hand as if in defense. "I didn't lure them over here. Promise. I was just cleaning up."

Janie shot a quick glance over her shoulder, as if to make sure her children were in the house, then turned back to Luke. "I'm sure you didn't, but at the same time, I would prefer it if you could keep your distance." She caught one corner of her mouth between her teeth, effectively ruining her lipstick, as if she was biting back other things she wanted to say.

"I understand your reluctance," he said, though he felt slightly annoyed. "But you don't need to worry about me around your kids."

"I think I'm a better judge of what to worry or not worry about. So just make sure you and that dog stay on your side of the fence, and we'll get along fine. Now if you'll excuse me, I have to go to church." Janie gave him a curt nod then left.

Bert came to stand beside him, watching Janie as she strode down the cracked and broken sidewalk to the house.

"She's kinda cute, ain't she?" he said with a grin.

"Yeah. Kinda," Luke conceded, though she'd be cuter if she didn't look at him like he was some kind of lecher or make Cooper sound like some kind of rabid animal.

"The other day that little boy was asking if he could help us. Said he knew how to pound nails real good." Bert laughed. "The little girl wanted to help, too. She reminded me of my own girl." Bert was quiet for a moment. "You got kids?"

"No. I don't." And to his surprise, the simple question raised a twinge of pain. Luke spun around. "Let's get back to work."

By early afternoon, Luke was feeling more confident about the progress of the job. If he hadn't been busy with that other house back in Calgary, he'd have been up here sooner. Obviously the crew needed the influence of the boss around to keep things going.

"So, anyone up for a coffee?" he said as the crew settled onto the deck for lunch.

"Black, two sugars," Dave said.

"Cream and one sugar," Bert said.

"Okay. I'll be back in a couple of minutes." Luke had seen a coffee shop on the main street when he'd scouted the town, and from the looks of the customers filling it, he figured it was one of the better places in town to grab a coffee.

He headed down the walk to the front of the house where his truck was parked, whistling. As he got in, he glanced over to the neighbor's house.

The flowerpots that Cooper had tossed over had been righted, but the plants in them looked broken and bedraggled.

He said he would replace them, and in spite of Janie's protests, he knew he had to do something.

Once he got things going far enough on the house, he'd take care of it.

"Why didn't you skip church to clean up?" Dodie called out from the back of the shop.

"I need church." Janie dipped the mop into the pail. "I need the nourishment I get there. My fellowship with fellow believers."

"And the serving coffee after church? Was that fellowship with fellow believers?" Dodie asked.

"I said I would help Mrs. Dodson."

"You could have skipped it, but of course, that wouldn't look good." Dodie dropped her pail of water on the table. "Janie Corbett is far too concerned with what other people might think if she possibly shirked even one second of what she perceived was her duty."

Janie didn't bother with a comeback. Dodie had never been one to care what people thought of her, and it showed both in the way she dressed and in the choices she made in her life.

"There are worse things you could accuse me of," Janie said, swishing the mop over the floor. She cocked one ear, listening for the kids. She heard Todd's muffled laughter and Autumn's singing. She guessed Suzie was with them.

"I also could accuse you of being too independent. If I hadn't been so nosy, I wouldn't have found out you were going to come here and clean all alone." Dodie's voice held an accusing note.

"I would have done this on my own."

"You would have been exhausted. Honestly, you don't have to do everything by yourself."

Why not? She'd fallen into that role out of necessity ever since she married Owen. Dependable and Owen were not words that belonged together.

"And I'm sure right now, you're hoping Mom doesn't find out you're working on a Sunday afternoon instead of having dinner with her." Dodie tut-tutted as she rinsed out a cloth and started wiping the tables.

"She won't if you keep your big yap shut."

"And your kids? What did you tell them to make sure they don't spill?"

"I told them Grandma wouldn't like it if she found out. Which, of course, meant I had to have a long conversation with Autumn about what would happen if Grandma did find out." She frowned at her sister. "Could you put the cinnamon and chocolate sprinkles on either side of the sugar container? And don't roll your eyes at me. This is my coffee shop and I like things in order."

"I'd think you have a lot more to be concerned about than sugar container placement." Dodie made a show of setting the containers in place, framing the scene with her hands then moving them a fraction to one side. "I can't believe you're still thinking of expanding. You have enough going as it is."

"I'm like a shark," Janie said. "I need to keep moving or die, which means I need to expand—" she stopped there. Her own father's business was successful mainly because he kept expanding, kept moving onward and upward. The only difference was Dan Westerveld didn't have a spouse who had gambled away all available equity in the house and business.

But Janie kept that information to herself. Neither her sister nor her parents knew how dire her financial situation was.

"What do you mean? And you're kind of struggling as it is."

"And that's why I need to expand. I'm just trying to make sure I can sustain my current lifestyle, which is hardly extravagant."

"I'll say. I can't believe that beater of a car of yours is still running."

"Regular maintenance helps." And prayer, Janie thought. Something she spent a lot of time on these days. "Although each time I bring it in for an oil change, they find something else wrong with it."

"You should marry a mechanic/carpenter. You wouldn't have to worry 'bout your car, or your house." Dodie moved to the next table.

"He should be a gardener, too," Janie muttered.

"I heard about your plants and that dog." Dodie's chuckle turned serious. "Did Autumn get over her scare?"

"She seems okay. Though I'm sure Todd will begin his dog campaign in earnest again."

"Mom said the dog's owner seemed a little odd."

"No odder than most," Janie replied, trying to sound disinterested. She was still a bit angry for the momentary tug of attraction she'd felt toward him.

But she'd set some firm boundaries this morning when she caught Todd talking to him. Start as you mean to go on.

"So I'm done with the tables. Now what?" Dodie swung the cloth back and forth as she looked around the shop.

"Maybe you could tidy up the storeroom and make sure my kids are behaving."

Dodie saluted and picked up her bucket.

While Dodie kept the kids entertained, Janie finished up, forcing herself to keep going. She was so incredibly weary, all she wanted to do, after church, was go home and sleep. But she had served squares at the anniversary tea, smiling and chatting and then dragged herself back here and kept going. Sometimes she felt as if she kept pushing her exhaustion into a box and sitting on the lid. One of these days it would all jump out and overwhelm her.

Dodie had accused her of being independent. But what else could she be? She had three children, and she was their sole caregiver. She had messed up once and was determined it would never happen again.

When she was finished with the floor, she brought the cleaning supplies back to the supply cupboard. And sighed. Dodie hadn't put the cloth back where it was supposed to be, nor was the cleaning solution capped.

If you want something done right, you've got to do it yourself, she thought, cleaning up behind her sister.

While she wiped out the pails and tidied up the rags, she heard Dodie and Todd talking to someone. She stepped out of the room in time to hear a familiar male voice.

Luke.

She pulled off the bandanna covering her head to fluff her hair, then stopped herself mid-primp.

What are you doing?

She retied her bandanna and strode out to the coffee shop area.

Luke stood just inside the doorway, laughing with Dodie. Sawdust sprinkled the burgundy corduroy shirt he wore tucked into faded jeans. He must have come right from the job site.

"Can I help you?" Janie asked, as she came nearer. Why had Dodie let him into the shop?

Luke glanced at Janie, and the smile animating his face slipped away.

"Sorry to bother you. Dodie just told me you're not open today."

"Not on Sundays." Janie wished she didn't sound so snippy, but she couldn't seem to keep that tone out of her voice around him.

He unsettled her, and she didn't like being unsettled.

"I just saw people inside and assumed you were open." Luke straightened. "I was hoping to get some coffee for my crew."

"Hey, Mr. Luke. Is Cooper in your truck?" Todd asked, pushing himself up so he could sit on one of the tables. "Can I see him?"

"I left him at home. I think he's done enough damage for a few days." Luke gave Todd a quick smile, his eyes drifting to Janie as if getting verification of that fact.

He was probably wondering if she was going to be issuing any more "stay away from my children" alerts.

She knew she had overreacted this morning, but she felt she had just cause. She didn't know him, and her previous neighbors had been a rowdy bunch that she'd had to constantly watch out for. One could hardly blame her for making sure he understood the boundaries.

And there was Autumn to think of.

"Mommy, I'm here." Autumn skipped into the coffee

shop, then stopped when she saw Luke. And promptly burst into tears.

Janie crouched down, taking her little girl into her arms. "Honey, what's wrong?"

Autumn sniffed, her head buried in Janie's neck. "Is the dog here?" she asked, the fear in her voice tugging at Janie's heart and reminding her again why she had cautioned Luke and his dog to stay away from her children.

"No honey. The dog is gone." She stroked Autumn's hair, wishing she had taken a bit more time to console her daughter yesterday. She truly thought she was okay.

Luke held up his hands. "Hey. I'm sorry. I had no idea the dog would be so rowdy. But he didn't hurt her. I saw him."

Janie gently smoothed the tears from her daughter's cheeks. "Do you want a pop?"

Autumn sniffed. "I love pop."

Janie knew. She seldom let her children have it; however, the situation required a bit of sweetening.

"Suzie, can you get Autumn a pop?"

"Can we have one, too?"

"Sure."

Todd jumped off the table, his interest in Luke trumped by the unexpected treat.

"I'll get them set up so they don't make a mess." Dodie turned her back on Luke as she gave her sister an arch look, which Janie ignored.

"I'm sorry. I can't get you anything," Janie said, turning back to Luke.

"Of course not. Can't be breaking the fourth commandment," he said, with a twinkle in his eye.

Her surprise must have shown on her face.

"Remember the Sabbath day, to keep it holy?" he prompted.

"I know the commandment," she said.

"But you're surprised that I do?" He effected a hurt look. "I used to go to church you know. You're not living next door to a perfect heathen."

"Used to go?" The phrase gave her a surprising sense of sadness.

"Yeah. When I lived with my foster father."

And didn't that little phrase create an intriguing hook?

"Mommy, Mommy, I made moose juice." Todd came running toward her, and Janie turned in time to see him trip over the leg of a table.

With a sense of inevitability, she watched pop arc out of his cup, then drop to the floor in a spectacular splash of reddish brown fluid.

"I'll get it," Dodie said, holding up a hand to stop her sister. "Don't even move."

But Janie was already on her knees, helping her son to his feet, checking him for pain and injury and trying to avoid the spreading sticky mess.

As she looked up, she caught Dodie smiling at Luke.

And Luke was smiling back.

She was surprised at the tiny hitch of disappointment. She knew this was how it should be. Owen had taught her some hard lessons. She had no right to be harboring any fantasies when it came to men.

She had the responsibility of her children, the emotional detritus of a messy marriage and a divorce. Keeping herself and her family independent of men was the only way to maintain control of her life.

"Mom, I'm sorry I spilled the pop," Todd said, "but can I have another one?"

Janie glanced at Todd's stained clothes, then did some

quick mental calculations. "Sorry, honey. We have to get back home so you can change, and then I have to take you to Cousin Ethan's farm right away. Otherwise I'll be late for Suzie's dance recital." If she didn't get Suzie to her recital, her mother, who had bought front row tickets as soon as they were on sale, would be disappointed. Again.

One step at a time, she reminded herself, doing the deep breathing exercise a friend had taught her the one time she made it to an exercise class. Relax.

Todd acknowledged this with a reluctant nod. "Maybe Cousin Ethan will have some pop for me."

"Maybe he will." Janie ruffled his hair, then called out to her sister. "I gotta get going, Dodie. Can you finish cleaning and then lock up?"

The only response she got was a giggle and then a belated, "Sure. I'll do that." It seemed Dodie's full attention was on Luke.

"Bye, Mr. Luke," Todd called out, tossing Luke a quick wave as Janie ushered them out the door.

"Bye, Todd," he called out. "See ya, Suzie, Autumn. See you later—"

Janie shut the back door, cutting off the rest of his farewell.

Chapter Three

Luke snapped open his ringing phone and glanced at the number as he spread the blueprint on the hood of his truck one-handed. Unknown name and number. Maybe the supplier he'd been trying to reach for the past few days.

"Hello. Luke here," he said, glancing at the specs for the electrician.

A pause. A breath, and then, "Hello, Luke. It's me. Your mom."

Luke straightened, anchoring the blueprint with one hand as frustration spiraled through him. "Hello, Lillian. Did you get the money?"

"Yes."

"That's good."

"Chuck tells me you're very busy on the house."

Uncle Chuck talks too much. "Yeah. I am."

A family walked past him. Mother holding a little boy's hand, father pushing the stroller. The perfect family.

Had his mother ever yearned for the same stability he had?

He shoved the thought aside. The only thing his mother had yearned for was another drink, another hit and another guy.

"So, I was thinking I could…maybe…" His mother heaved a sigh. "I wanna see you."

Luke wondered why she still bothered. The last time she'd asked, like a sucker, he'd agreed. He'd waited an hour, then had gone back to the hotel he'd been staying at. He should have known better. Ever since he'd moved to Al's, she'd try to visit him at least once a year. And once a year, he'd wait.

"Sorry. I'm busy."

"Too busy for your mom?"

You don't know how a mom behaves, Luke thought, glancing at the house beside his. As if his thoughts summoned her, Janie came outside with a watering can, Autumn trailing behind her. Janie pulled a plant from a hook and set it down so her little girl could water it.

That's what mothers are like, Luke thought, melancholy surging through him.

Janie glanced his way and lifted her hand in a little neighborly wave.

He nodded, still holding on to the blueprint with one hand, his phone with the other. Still holding on to the connection he had with the woman who was his mother, but didn't know how motherhood worked.

"If you need more money, just say so," Luke said, wishing he could just hang up.

Silence greeted that remark.

"I gotta go," he said finally. "If you need anything, please talk to Uncle Chuck."

"Okay. Bye."

He waited for her to disconnect, then closed his phone, watching Janie finish the job with her little girl, waiting until they went inside.

He folded up the blueprint and as he walked to his house, he glanced at his watch.

Twenty minutes left. The guys had promised to stay until six-thirty today. He was just about to go inside the house when his phone rang again.

It was his uncle.

"Hey, what's up?" he asked, a smile on his face. Talking to his uncle was the perfect antidote for the phone call he'd just had.

They made some chitchat. Discussed Luke's financial situation (okay for now), his girlfriend situation (nonexistent) and then his uncle fell silent.

Luke had a premonition about what was coming next.

"Just talked to Lillian," Chuck said.

I'm good, Luke thought. "I already gave her the money."

"I don't think that's what she wants, Luke."

"It's all she's ever wanted from anyone." Even his foster father, Al, had been subjected to Lillian's pleas for "just a bit of cash to tide me over."

"I think it would be good for you if you could see her. I think it would be good for her, too. You know the Lord tells us to forgive seventy times seven."

Luke pressed his index finger to his temple, massaging away a potential headache. "You know, Uncle Chuck? I really think I've passed that amount a few years ago."

"Have you? Have you truly prayed and felt forgiveness for her four hundred and ninety times?"

Chuck's quiet question raised, once again, the twisted mixture of guilt and anger he felt when he thought of his mother. The anger was justified, and he knew the guilt was misplaced. She had been the one who had left him alone again and again. She had been the one with the false promises each time to turn her life around. He couldn't give her any more of his time and energy.

Money, though? That he could give her. "Tell her I'm busy. Out of town. Just keep her away from me."

"I'll do what you are asking. But I do want you to know I still pray that you and she can come to have some kind of relationship."

Each time his uncle phoned or e-mailed Luke, it was with the promise that he would pray for his lost sheep nephew and Luke's mother.

Luke drew in a long, slow breath. "Maybe you could pray I get this house done on time so I don't lose my initial investment."

"I keep praying for you, my boy. And not for that house."

"Thanks, Uncle Chuck. I mean that." He said goodbye, and as Luke closed his cell phone, he felt again the curious feeling that he had let his uncle down. Luke knew his uncle was disappointed that Luke didn't go to church and was even more disappointed that he didn't allow Lillian into his life.

He didn't know, he thought. He just didn't know what it had been like. Al had, but Al was gone.

Luke slipped the phone into the holder on his belt and turned his mind back to the house.

"So, what's next?" Bert sauntered over, his hammer swinging in his belt loop. Cooper trotted alongside him, his attention focused laserlike on the man.

Against Luke's wishes, Bert had given Cooper half his sandwich at lunchtime, and since then, Cooper had followed him around with unbridled optimism.

Luke's gaze ticked over the exterior of the house. "I think we'll start yarding the shingles off the north side of the roof and pray it doesn't rain."

"Not a praying man," Bert said with a grin as he absently

petted Cooper's head. "But I'll ask the missus. She talks to God from time to time."

Luke was tempted to ask Bert to ask the missus to put in a good word for him, as well. His uncle's phone call had reminded him of Todd's simple comment Sunday morning. And Janie's surprise that he knew which of the commandments concerned keeping the Sabbath.

In spite of her anger with him and Cooper, he found himself thinking about her and her family quite a bit. Wondered if there was a man somewhere in the picture.

"What in the world is she trying to do?" Bert pointed in the direction of Janie's house.

The woman, who had just been on Luke's mind, was perched atop a wobbly wooden ladder that looked more rickety than her porch steps.

"That ladder is going to bust for sure," Bert said, shaking his head. "We should get her one of ours."

Luke didn't want to get involved. The boundaries between the two yards had been laid out enough times for him that crossing them would only prove his idiocy.

He turned back to his blueprints.

"Whoa, that doesn't look good," Bert said, clapping his hand on his hard hat.

Luke spun around again in time to see the ladder wobble as Janie caught her balance by hanging on to the gutter with one hand, the other pressed against the wall of the house. The ladder was barely upright, but she managed to get it steadied. The bright yellow bandanna holding her hair back slipped over her eyes, and she let go of the gutter to straighten it. Her white shirt had smudges of dirt, which made Luke wonder what else she'd been doing earlier in the evening.

"Mommy, are you okay?" Todd's concerned voice was Luke's undoing. Janie might not like him interfering, but if something happened to her that he could have prevented, especially if it happened in front of her son, he couldn't live with himself.

"That woman needs help," Bert said, shaking his head. "Maybe I should head over there—"

"You guys get going on that roof. I'll bring a ladder over," Luke said with a sigh of inevitability. "Cooper, stay," he commanded.

Which of course made Cooper more curious than obedient. And as Luke ran to the fence, Cooper followed.

"Stay here," Luke commanded, his voice even more stern. He waited until he saw Cooper sit, then climbed the fence crossing the sacred boundary.

But before he could get to Janie, she let go of the gutter and took another step up the ladder.

The step splintered under her weight, her foot came down and she landed on her chest on the top rung. The ladder swayed and would have gone over, if he hadn't grabbed it, steadied it and pushed it upright.

His heart pounded in his chest. She had come so close to seriously hurting herself.

"Hey, Luke," Todd called out from the back of the yard where he was sitting on the grass, reading a book. Autumn had been swinging on a swing set that looked as sketchy as the ladder he was holding up. But she stopped, staring at him. "Are you helping my mommy?"

Janie straightened and glanced down. Startled, she said, "I didn't see you…you should have said…" She took a breath, then caught the gutter again.

"Don't hang on to that," Luke said. "It's not strong enough."

"Well, I don't know what else to hang on to." But she let go and placed both hands on the wall of the house.

"Get down from there. You're going to do serious damage to yourself," Luke said.

"Where's Autumn?" Janie asked, her gaze narrowing as she glanced over at Luke's yard.

And why was she worried about Autumn when she had just had a near-death experience herself?

Luke followed the direction of her gaze only to see Cooper with his front paws on the top of the teetering fence, watching the scene unfold with avid interest.

"Hey, Cooper. Good to see you," Todd called out, putting his book down and walking toward the dog.

"Cooper. Down," Luke called out, not trusting the strength of the fence.

Cooper barked. The fence shook.

And Autumn started to cry.

"Bert, get that dog away from the fence," Luke called out as Janie clambered down the rest of the ladder, then ran to her daughter's side to comfort her.

Bert ran over to Cooper and pulled him down. "Should I tie him up?"

Luke sighed. He had just finished cleaning up the yard so that his dog could run free. "Yeah. I guess."

As Bert pulled a very reluctant Cooper toward the trailer to tie him up, Luke folded up the wooden ladder, surprised to see his hands still shaking.

"What are you doing?" Janie demanded as she carried Autumn to the house. "I'm not done."

"I'm going to get you a new ladder. This one isn't safe." Luke set the ladder on its side. "And then I'm going to be the one going up it to clean the gutters."

"There's no need. I was taking care of it." Autumn wriggled on Janie's hip, and Janie set her down. "Suzie, can you please come out here and get your sister," she called out.

"I'm not done with my homework," Suzie called back from inside the house.

Janie sighed and pressed her fingertips to her temples as if she was holding something back. "Todd, can you take Autumn inside? You can play a game with her if you want."

Todd, who was hanging over the fence, watching Cooper, reluctantly pulled away and trudged across the yard. He picked up his book, then held out his hand to his sister. "C'mon Autumn. What do you want to play?" he asked as he led her up the porch steps and into the house.

Janie turned back to Luke and gave him a smile that he could only describe as insincerely sweet. "If I could borrow a ladder from you, then I can finish the job and you can get back to your work."

How convenient. She could borrow his tools, but he couldn't set foot in her yard.

"I'd hate to disappoint you," he said, his voice growing chilly, "but you're not going to finish the job. I'm going to finish the job. Using my ladder."

"I'm perfectly capable," she protested, her blue eyes snapping. "I've done it before. You don't need to be here."

The remnants of the fear he'd experienced when he saw her near miss pushed his guard down.

He took a step closer, his voice growing quiet so the kids couldn't hear.

"You just about killed yourself in front of your children just a few moments ago." His anger was building as her eyes narrowed. "If you're the responsible and concerned mother that you seem to be, then you won't go anywhere near those gutters."

Janie's mouth opened then shut again. She looked like she was on the verge of a coronary, but Luke didn't care.

"So why don't you go inside where you'll be safe from me and my dog," he continued, pressing his momentary advantage, "and I'll get the proper tools to do this job."

Janie opened her mouth once more, but Luke didn't stick around to hear her tell him again how she could do it herself.

He was halfway across the yard when a thought hit him. Following this hunch, he turned around and walked back to the wooden ladder she was struggling to pick up. Without a word, he took it from her as easily as he would a toy and carried it back to the fence.

"That's mine," she called out as he tossed it into his yard. "I got that ladder from my dad. It's an heirloom."

He didn't acknowledge her comments as he hopped the fence but had to laugh at her last comment. *Heirloom* indeed. Fossil would be more apt.

He strapped on his pouch, grabbed a cordless drill and screws, slipped on his gloves and picked up an aluminum ladder on his way back to Janie's yard.

He put the ladder over the fence and hopped over again, knowing that this route would give Janie less time to come up with some kind of alternate scheme to keep him away from her precious gutters.

By the time he got back to the house, Janie seemed to have calmed down. She even gave him a smile when he opened up the ladder.

"You know I can—"

"Forget it," Luke said as he scrambled up the ladder.

The gutter was plugged solid, and it took him a few minutes to pull out all the leaves and mud. They musn't have been cleaned for years.

While he worked, Janie stayed at the bottom of the ladder, watching. He felt like telling her there was nothing worth stealing up here, not with the shape her roof was in, but he kept his smart comment to himself.

When he was done with this part of the gutters, he fitted the screws to the dilapidated metal and spun them in with the drill.

"You're going to have to replace these in the next year or so." He tightened the last of the screws.

"I'm not surprised," she answered. "How do the shingles look, or do I not want to ask?"

Luke tested the gutter. When he was satisfied, he gave the roof a quick glance. About one-fourth of the shingles were lifting off and curling up. "Bad news there, too."

"Again. Not surprised."

What did surprise him was the faint smile curving her lips as he came down the ladder.

He liked the smile better than the glower she had given him a few moments ago.

"I'm sorry about snapping at you before," she said as he folded up the ladder. "It's just I think I got a bit of a scare myself when I almost fell." She sighed as she rubbed her arms, "Anyway, thanks."

He waved her comment away. "I'm not done yet," he said picking up the ladder and moving it a few feet over. "There's a few more yards of gutter to clean."

"You don't have to do all that," she began. Then stopped when he held up his gloved hand yet again. "Okay. Okay. But let me get you something to drink when you're done. Iced tea okay?"

"Iced tea would be great."

She nodded and went back into the house. While he worked, he could hear her talking to Todd and Autumn. He heard the refrigerator door open, then the hum of voices and the scent of food, which made his mouth water and made him think of the cold pizza he was going to heat up for supper. A minute later, Janie poked her head out the door. "You still doing okay?"

"Still doing just fine," he replied.

He felt a moment's nostalgia as he scraped and cleaned. In the kitchen he could hear Janie talking to the kids, and he wondered about her husband. Did he come home looking forward to being with them? Did the kids run to greet him?

Would he ever experience that?

Now would be a good time to get off the self-pity express. Sure he wanted a family some day. Sure he'd been waiting for that to happen. But it would in time and with the right woman, if he ever settled in one place long enough.

An hour later, he was folding up the ladder when the porch door opened and Janie came out carrying a frosted glass of the promised iced tea.

He stripped off his gloves and as he took the glass, the ice cubes clinked against the side.

"Are you done?" Janie asked, hugging herself against the evening chill settling into the yard.

"Yep. I tightened the hangers on the other side of the house. They should be good for awhile yet." Luke took a sip of his iced tea then pointed his glass at the swing set. "I think you might want to look at replacing that too."

Janie frowned as she glanced at the dilapidated set. "It's okay. I got it from a neighbor."

"For now. But one of these days Autumn or Todd will fall on their behind when they sit down on it."

"Well, I don't think they need another one."

"Don't you want to do what's best for the kids?"

Janie gave him a knowing look. "What's best for my kids is always first and foremost on my mind. And right now, that swing set is perfectly fine. I wouldn't have it in my yard if it wasn't safe."

Luke merely arched his eyebrows and glanced over at the spot in the fence where he had dumped the ladder.

Janie seemed to know exactly where his mind went. "And I never let the kids on the ladder, in case you must know."

"I don't *need* to know, but it is good to know."

He gave her a quick smile, pleased to see a glimmer of a smile.

He took another sip of iced tea as he stood on her porch, wondering what she had made for supper that smelled so good. He liked cooking, when he had the time. He just never had much of it—time that was.

Asking would put her in an awkward position. She would never ask him in for supper, and nor should she, so he didn't broach the subject.

He took another sip of the cool drink, suddenly loath to leave Janie and the house with the kids inside and the sounds and smells of a home surrounding him like a tanta-lizing dream.

Somewhere down the street someone was barbecuing, and beyond that he heard the muffled buzz of a lawn mower. His thoughts cast back to the precious years he had with Al, the closest he had ever come to real family life.

Cooper's bark brought him back to the here and now.

He should get going. He looked over at Janie, who was watching him. Then, to his surprise and, he had to admit, pleasure, a flush crept up her neck and she looked down. She pushed a wave of hair back from her face, then reached into the back pocket of her worn jeans. "Thanks again for all your work," she said, pulling out a handful of bills.

Luke felt as chilled as the ice in his drink. "I don't want your money."

"You don't have to sound so angry. It's perfectly legitimate to pay someone for doing work."

"I did it because I wanted to help you out."

"I don't want to be in your debt," she said, pushing the money at him. "This way we're even."

Luke knew all he had to do was walk away without taking the money. But he gave that another thought. Janie was an independent sort, that much he'd surmised from the few times he'd spoken to her.

A single mother, beholden, so to speak, to a single man.

Maybe it would be better if he took the money and swallowed his own pride for the sake of hers.

He downed the last of his iced tea and handed her the glass. "I usually charge about thirty bucks an hour for custom work. I put in an hour."

"That's too cheap."

"So now you're going to dicker over the cost?" He laughed in spite of his frustration with her.

"I just want to be fair." Her quick smile made him realize he had done the right thing in taking her money. Boundaries and all that.

And he especially appreciated the smile.

"Thirty bucks is more than fair."

Janie counted out one twenty and two fives.

As Luke pocketed the money, he looked down at the deck. "You might want to have this looked at as well," he said, pointing with the toe of his heavy work boot at a rotting board.

"I look at it enough," Janie said, with a feeble laugh. "But thanks again for your help."

"No problem." He gathered his tools and walked back toward the fence.

When he was on the other side, he looked back at the house, but she was already inside her house. Safe and cozy with her family.

At least he had Cooper, he thought, bringing the ladder back to the house. The dog was a poor conversationalist but a faithful friend.

He untied Cooper and the dog ran back to the fence as if hoping to find the kids. Once again, he planted his paws on the fence, and Luke watched with a sense of inevitability as the fence gave way and Cooper fell with it.

"Cooper. Come here," he called, running over to catch the dog before he jumped into Janie's yard.

He'd just earned some major brownie points with his neighbor. He certainly didn't want the dog to jeopardize that.

Cooper ran back to him and danced around him, eager to play. Luke felt bad because the poor dog had been tied up again.

Luke picked up a wooden stake and tossed it across the yard. Cooper launched himself after it, his long legs scrabbling for purchase on the ground. He picked it up and ran back dropping it at Luke's feet.

They kept it up for a few minutes; though Cooper could have gone on until he dropped, Luke was hungry.

He straightened and sent one last look toward the house. He saw two faces looking out from one of the windows of the house. Todd and Autumn.

Todd was smiling, and to Luke's surprise, Autumn was as well.

He waved and the kids waved back. When Cooper came back to him with the stick, he saw Autumn point at them both, then laugh.

It bothered him that this little girl appeared so afraid of his dog. Cooper had such a good heart and he sensed, given the chance, she might appreciate him as well.

And then he had an idea.

Chapter Four

Carry the two and add four and no matter how she worked it, her amazing plan would require a lot of work. And cash input.

Janie pushed her hands through her hair, wishing away the number on the computer screen of her laptop. She had to have punched something in wrong.

With a sigh, she started checking her figures, fully aware of the ticking clock. She only had a few more minutes before she had to take Suzie to dance practice. But she had to get this right before she brought it to Mr. Chernowyk. She was counting on this audacious plan to shift her financial circumstances.

"Mom. Company."

Janie's heart sunk as she pulled her attention away from the blinking cursor on the computer screen. She simply did not have time for company.

"Who is it, Todd?" she called back.

"The dog man is here. Luke."

Luke? What in the world could he want now?

As Janie walked out of the kitchen, she picked up a book Todd had left on the steps and set it on a side table.

The front door was open and silhouetted against the light

from the outside, was Luke, aka the dog man, holding something in his hands.

"Is Cooper with you?" Todd asked him.

"He's tied up on your front deck."

"Can I go pet him?"

Luke glanced at Janie. "Is it okay?"

Janie tried to mentally shift gears, almost feeling a grinding sound in her head. Her mind still back in the debits and credits columns of her bookkeeping program, but when she saw Luke, standing in the doorway of her house, she felt a tremor of anticipation.

"Sorry, Todd. You need to change. We have to leave in a few minutes." She hoped Luke would get the hint and realize that she had another schedule to keep.

"But Mom, my clothes are still clean."

Janie raised one eyebrow in his direction. Todd sighed but thankfully did as he was told. Todd was her little trouper. Always obedient, always doing what he was supposed to do. Which balanced out the challenges she was having with Suzie.

Through the thin ceiling, she heard Suzie's feet storming around above her. When Janie came back from the coffee shop, she was the happy recipient of Suzie's foul mood. Her daughter had accused her mother of causing everything evil in her life up until now and possibly including global warming and the boll weevil. She didn't want to go to dance practice tonight.

In fact, she didn't want to do anything but hibernate in her room, her stereo blasting while she complained on the phone to her friends about her horrible mother who wouldn't let her get private Internet access and her own computer.

She turned her attention back to Luke.

"I brought you a peace offering," he said, holding up a pot of brightly colored and unusual looking flowers. "The guy at the greenhouse said they were some kind of new and improved be-something or other." Luke continued. "Of course, he could tell me anything. I know squat about flowers."

"Begonia, I'm guessing," Janie said. She was about to protest the gift, but he handed it to her and she had no choice but to take it. The yellow-hooded blooms didn't look familiar. The greenhouse must have received a new shipment.

"I replaced the pots at the end of the sidewalk as well. I know they're not original and rare or anything like that, but I thought they looked like the ones you had."

"You didn't have to do that," she protested.

"Oh, yes, I did. Have you seen those plants? There wasn't much left to them."

"I was going to replace them," she said.

"Now you don't have to. I said I was going to replace them, so I did. The greenhouse guy gave me some instructions on what to do with them, but I forgot. I figured you, with your green thumb, would know."

"But I can't pay you back."

"Don't even think about that. It was my dog that wrecked them."

While he spoke, Autumn came thumping down the stairs on her behind, dragging her bear.

Janie glanced over her shoulder, suddenly concerned. Would she cry when she saw Luke again?

Autumn blinked and hugged her teddy bear, her eyes going past him as if to check to see if his lunatic pooch was anywhere in the vicinity.

To Janie's surprise, Luke slowly squatted, his knees cracking. "Hey there, Autumn. How are you?" he said.

Autumn stared at him, then she carefully smiled. "I'm good. How are you?"

"I'm fine. What's your teddy bear's name?"

Autumn hugged her bear tighter. "Berry Bear. I had him since I was little. Where's your dog?" she asked, a hint of fear in her voice.

At her question, Luke pushed himself to his feet, his expression growing serious as he turned to Janie.

"I want to run this past you, but it really bugs me that your girl is so afraid of dogs. I was wondering if I could try something."

Cooper barked, and Autumn jumped again.

"Can you come with me outside a minute?" Luke asked.

"Are you going to be okay?" Janie asked her young daughter.

Autumn nodded, still clutching her bear.

Janie closed the door behind her and sidestepped the exuberant dog that jumped up, then barked.

"Cooper. Stop it," she said, her voice stern. "Sit."

The dog dropped to his haunches, his head cocked to one side, his eyes fixed on her.

Luke shook his head in wonderment. "How do you do that?"

Janie wasn't sure herself why Cooper had listened to her. "Maybe it's my 'mom' voice," she suggested.

"You're going to have to teach me," he said.

"What's this about, Luke?"

"Like I said, it bugs me so bad that Autumn is afraid of my dog." Luke patted Cooper's head absently. "We're going to be next door for awhile, and Cooper is going to be running around in the yard next to yours. I don't want her to be scared of him."

"And how do you hope to fix that?"

Luke scratched his forehead with his index finger. "Well, would you let her come outside right now? I'm sure if we give her a chance to see the dog, on her own, take her time, maybe she could see he's okay?"

Janie bit her lip, looking back at the house, her concern for her daughter overriding Luke's request.

"I know he's a bit hyper, but he's all heart. He just gets excited when he's in a new place."

The earnestness in his voice struck a peculiar chord with her. Why did he care? And why did it matter to him that Autumn like his dog?

"I don't think that's necessary—"

"C'mon, Janie. If she doesn't start on this, she's going to spend the next month sitting on the deck, afraid to go farther into her own yard."

His eyes held hers, and then he gave her a crooked smile.

Don't let him weasel his way into your life, she could almost hear her mother say as she let his smile ease away one tiny part of the barrier she had been determined to put up against him.

Then she glanced at Cooper. He sat quietly on the step, his head cocked to one side as if pleading with her to love him.

She didn't know what to do.

"We can wait, but I thought the sooner we get this done, the better."

"Okay, but if she shows the least bit of apprehension, I want you to get that dog away as fast as possible."

"Of course." He sounded aggrieved, but she didn't care. Her first priority was her child's well-being.

She stepped inside the house just as Suzie came down the stairs.

"Autumn, do you want to come with me outside?" she asked.

"What's outside?" Suzie interjected, walking to the front door. "Hey, it's Luke and Cooper."

"Suzie, do you mind staying inside? I'd like to take Autumn out by herself."

Her oldest daughter shot her an annoyed look. "But I want to see Cooper," she said as she opened the door.

"Please, can you stay in the house? Luke and I want to try something with Autumn," Janie said, trying to placate her daughter.

"Why does Autumn always get all the attention?" Suzie hissed.

Can you say overreact? Janie stifled a sigh, praying, as she always did, for patience with Suzie.

"Please, Suzie, it isn't that big a deal. Just wait, and you can come out later."

"Okay. Fine." She walked to the living room and dropped onto the couch.

Janie reached her hand out to Autumn. "Honey, can you come with me?"

Autumn hugged her bear closer, but nodded, getting up from the stairs. Janie took her hand and slowly opened the door.

"Hi, Mr. Luke." Autumn's voice grew quiet, her eyes fixed on Cooper.

"Hey, girly. You remember Cooper, don't you?"

Autumn nodded. "I'm scared of that dog."

"He's kinda big, isn't he?" Luke asked. "Remember when he came to your house before?"

She nodded again, her expression solemn.

"What did he do?"

"He ran into the house. And drank out of the toilet."

Janie couldn't help but smile at her daughter's memory. Luke glanced up, sharing her humor. Then he sent her a wink before turning his attention back to Autumn.

"You know, Cooper thinks you're cute."

This caught her attention. "How do you know?"

"See how he's looking at you?"

And sure enough, Cooper's attention was fixed on Autumn again, as if he was trying to say something.

"Would you come and tell him that he's a handsome dog? He'd like that." Luke asked.

Autumn looked up at her mother. Fear flashed across her face, but in her eyes Janie caught the faintest glimmer of hope.

"Why don't you try, honey?" Janie said, keeping her voice quiet. Nonthreatening. "Maybe he'll say something to you."

Autumn's gaze ticked from Janie, to Luke, then back to Cooper. Janie took her daughter's hand, but waited for her to make the first move.

Cooper whined, shifted his huge feet and stayed sitting. Luke wasn't holding him back, the leash was slack; however, he kept a tight grip on the end just in case.

Luke knelt down beside his dog as Autumn took her first step. Then another. Cooper leaned just a bit forward, as if encouraging her.

"He doesn't bite, does he?" Autumn asked, her voice a tiny sound that cut at Janie's heart. But, at the same time, she knew this was a good thing Luke was doing.

"Cooper never bites anyone. He wants to be everyone's friend."

Autumn took another step, still clinging to Janie.

"Well, I think that's a good start," Luke said, touching Autumn on the shoulder.

Autumn's smile gave Janie hope.

Cooper whined and got to his feet. Autumn took a step back but the terror seemed to have eased somewhat.

Janie hated to break the moment, hated to be "the mom"

again, but time was ticking. "Autumn, you should go into the house and change. We have to leave in a few minutes."

Autumn gave Cooper one more glance, then bounced back into the house. As Janie watched her go, she felt a glimmer of hope. Though she never wanted a pet herself, her daughter's fear of them was a concern every time they came near a dog. Maybe with time it would go away.

"Thanks for doing this," Janie said. "I really appreciate that."

"It's just a small start." Luke shifted his weight, loosening his grip on the leash. "I'm glad this goofy dog seems to get that he needs to be careful with her."

Janie looked up at Luke, surprised to see him looking down at her, a faint smile teasing the corner of his mouth. For a moment, their gazes held and Janie felt a shift in her breathing as she caught a glimpse of interest in his gaze. And she felt herself drawn into it.

Suzie's raised voice from inside the house brought her tumbling back to reality. Widow. Mother. Three children.

"I have to go," she said, making her tone abrupt. "Let me know what those flowers cost, and I can pay you back."

And before Luke could protest, she stepped back into the house.

Chapter Five

✦

And how was she supposed to pay him back for that?

Janie looked out her kitchen window, the shirt she was folding clutched against her chest. She was sure the new fence hadn't been up this morning when she and the kids were having breakfast. Of course, she could have missed Luke working on it between tossing clothes into the washing machine, making lunches and trying to convince Suzie that the outfit she desperately wanted to wear to school wasn't suitable.

In the end Janie had caved, rationalizing that she had to choose the battles she wanted to win. And fights about clothing fell below unsuitable friends and parties—two potential minefields waiting over the horizon. She often wondered if she and Autumn would someday have the same strained relationship. She also wondered if Suzie had absorbed some of the resentments Janie had carried throughout her pregnancy.

"I'm going to start the movie." Dodie poked her head in the kitchen. "Need some help with the laundry?"

Janie waved her sister off. "I'm just about done."

"If you would have let me help, you could have been done and we both would be slouching on your bed eating popcorn and dissing the actors."

"Why don't you go ahead and get a head start on the dissing? I have to zip next door to pay Luke back for the flowers he replaced."

Dodie gave her sister a knowing smile. "Don't zip on my account."

The hopeful note in her sister's voice was hard to ignore. "I'll only be gone a couple of minutes," she said as she placed Autumn's shirt on the pile.

"If you're not back when the movie is over, I'll be sleeping on the bed."

Janie pulled the cash out of her purse, then walked to the window. And sighed.

The prestained boards, marching in a straight line dividing the two properties called to the part of Janie's heart that appreciated order and neatness. But while she was relieved that Luke had replaced the sagging and dangerous fence, she was keenly aware that she couldn't repay him for it. Not yet.

Maybe you don't have to pay him back. Maybe he just did it because he wanted to.

She quelled the pernicious voice. Of course she would repay him. That was how things were done. She'd have to figure out a way to do it, but there was no way she was going to be in his debt.

For now, she had enough to pay him for the flowers. She headed out the door, careful to avoid the rotting steps on the back stairs and trying to relegate that particular task to another time and another day.

There was no answer at the trailer when she knocked. Luke's truck was parked in front of the house, so she figured he was around somewhere. She paused, then followed the sound of hammering coming from the upstairs of the house.

She knocked on the front door, then stepped inside.

Her first impression was dust and dirt and the tang of freshly cut wood. Her next, chaos.

A lift of lumber lay on the worn rug in the middle of the hallway facing her, and through a set of sliding glass doors set in the wall to her left and hazy with dust, she saw drop cloths on the floor. A ladder leaned up against a wall with an arched doorway leading to another room. Chunks of drywall and pieces of wood lay heaped on sheets of plastic covering the living room floor.

Through the doorway ahead of her, she saw what she presumed was the kitchen. A horizontal stripe of bright yellow paint halfway up the wall showed where the kitchen cabinets had once been. Chunks of drywall were scattered over the floor here as well. One wall had been reduced to studs with the wiring showing.

The hammering stopped and she heard Cooper's deep-chested bellow resonating from upstairs, announcing her arrival.

This was followed by the sound of paws thumping down the stairs. Cooper came skittering around the corner, raising dust and heading straight toward her.

"Sit, you big beast," she commanded in her firmest voice, bracing herself for the canine onslaught.

To her surprise, Cooper stopped dead in his tracks, dust surrounding him like a cloud, looking at her with a quizzical glance, his tail wagging slowly.

"Sit," she commanded again.

And he dropped onto his haunches, still watching her as if awaiting further instructions.

"Who's there?" Luke called out.

"It's uh, Janie from next door."

She heard the jangling chimes of a cell phone, then Luke was coming down the stairs. He was scowling as he spoke into the phone. His frown combined with the dark slash of his eyebrows and the stubble on his cheeks gave him a menacing look.

But when he saw her a smile transformed his face.

Janie wished she didn't feel that tremble in her heart, that faint fluttering.

Luke covered the phone. "I'll just be a minute," he said, then turned away, his features set in unexpected hard lines that created an air of tension and discomfort. Janie felt suddenly awkward and wished she hadn't come.

"No, Lillian, I don't have time to visit you," he was saying. "I'm too busy."

Lillian. And he was too busy to see her. Why did that thought give her a moment of cheer?

"No. Please don't call again." Luke waited a moment and glanced over at Janie as if making sure she was still there. He gave her a wan smile, then turned his attention back to his phone. "Sorry. I have to go. I have someone here. Bye." Then he closed the phone and shoved it in his pocket. He gave Janie an apologetic look. "Sorry about that. My mother."

And he called her Lillian.

"I'm sorry," Janie said. "I shouldn't have just stopped in. I hope you didn't cut the call off on my account."

Luke waved off her comment. "I didn't have much to say to her."

Janie knew she shouldn't pry, but she couldn't help herself. "I thought you were raised by a foster father."

"I was. I moved in with Al when I was twelve."

"So it wasn't because you didn't have parents."

"Well, technically I had a father and a mother," Luke corrected, unbuckling his tool belt. "Apparently my father died when I was three, and he never knew I existed. And though I lived with her until I was twelve, my mom often seemed to feel the same."

Though he tossed the words out as if they meant nothing, Janie sensed an underlying hurt tinged with bitterness. She tried to imagine him a young boy alone and felt a stab of pity. She wanted to ask more but hesitated. Finding out about Luke's past would create a connection.

"Enough about that," he said, his gaze shifting to her. "What brings you here?"

Janie thought of the money in her pocket and remembered Luke's reaction the last time she tried to pay him.

"I can show you around the place if you want," Luke continued.

Janie removed her hand from her pocket. "I don't want to interrupt your work," she said, though her heart wasn't in it. She did want to see the house. And, though she didn't want to examine her motives too hard, she wanted Luke to show her.

"It was time to quit anyhow."

Janie glanced around the house again. "I've always wondered what this house looked like on the inside," she said. "When we first moved to this neighborhood, this place was for sale, but it was out of our price range."

"We, being you and your husband?" Luke asked.

Janie nodded, slipping her hands in her pockets, her one hand sliding past the bills she had tucked inside—her real reason for being here. She pulled her hand out again.

"We didn't even look inside, but I loved the style. And the huge backyard of course. I must admit, I envied the backyard."

"The house has tons of potential," Luke agreed. "And thanks to the previous owners, it needs tons of work."

"I've always wondered how one would go about doing a ton of work."

"Lots of heavy lifting," Luke replied, a twinkle kindling in his eyes.

"I'm glad to see that it's getting fixed up. The previous owners were a bit rowdy and, well—"

"Weren't friends of Jesus, I understand."

Janie frowned.

"Todd told me. Last Sunday. He said the people who lived here drank and that you told him they weren't friends of Jesus."

Her frown switched to a laugh. "I forgot about that. They certainly liked their parties."

"Yeah. Not hard to tell the way they treated this house." Luke ran his hand over the pitted railing of the stairs, as if soothing away the abuse. "Shame really."

"But you're going to restore it to its former glory," Janie said.

"Hopefully I can get it done by the time my partner wants the open house."

"I understand you've done this before," Janie said, as she slid open the glass doors to the living room. The space opened up in front of her. To her left, a bay window overlooked the front lawn, and directly ahead of her, two windows flanked the large brick fireplace.

"I've done this six times before."

Janie heard it again. The same touch of melancholy. "Don't you get tired of it? Fixing up places, making them into homes, only to sell them again?" she asked as she walked over to the bay window, Cooper padding along beside her. The cushion of the window seat was torn and covered with drywall dust, but Janie sat down anyway. The familiar street looked different from this angle. It made her feel a little disoriented.

She realized Luke hadn't answered her question. She

glanced over at him only to see him leaning in the doorway, watching her.

Their gazes caught. Held.

For a moment something indefinable, yet appealing, flickered between them. She swallowed as her heart quickened ever so slightly. His dark hair, dark eyebrows and the stubble creating interesting shadows on his high cheekbones and strong chin had morphed from menacing to appealing.

No. Don't even venture into that territory, focusing her attention back to her children.

When Owen started staying away, she had vowed that after her relationship with the Lord, Suzie, Autumn and Todd would always be her first priority. Above Owen. Above any man.

Janie turned her attention to Cooper, petting him.

"You don't seem to mind my dog so much now," Luke said, coming to sit beside her in the window.

Janie swallowed at his nearness, but moving now would look like she was running away from him. Like she was scared of the feelings he was rousing in her.

"I'm glad that Autumn was willing to see him," Luke continued.

I should go, Janie thought. I should give him the money and get back to my house as fast as I can.

Since Owen left, she had never spent time by herself in the company of a single, attractive man. She didn't have time to date and, truth be told, the lessons she learned from Owen were ones she didn't want to repeat.

But with Luke she felt different. She felt the whisper-like touch of hope.

"I want to thank you again," she said quietly. "Like you said, it will take time for her to get over her fear completely."

"What happened to make her so frightened?"

Janie rubbed her arms as the memories slipped back.

"Unless you don't want to tell me," he said.

She shook her head. "No. I don't mind. It would explain a few things for you." She wrapped her arms around her midsection, her mind casting back to that horrible day.

"Owen had brought a dog home. I've never been fond of dogs. Been a bit afraid of them myself, if I were to be honest. But I thought it would be good for the kids. The dog was a bit hyper—"

"Like Cooper," Luke interjected.

"Actually, worse. But Owen kept assuring me he would settle down. Then one day, Owen was between jobs and he was supposed to be watching Autumn while I was shopping with Suzie and Todd. He fell asleep, and the next thing he knew, Autumn was screaming. The dog had bitten her."

"How did that happen?"

Janie looked away, hugging herself as if trying to hold the memory in. "I never did get a straight story from Owen, but I understood when Autumn went to pet the dog, he jumped on her and bit her on the leg. Right through her pants. Took fifteen stitches to sew up the gash."

Janie shuddered, remembering far too easily the frantic rush to the hospital. Her call to her mother. The blood pouring down Autumn's leg and the fitful crying that tore at Janie's heart.

"I had just started up the coffee shop, so of course I felt immediately deluged with guilt. Should never have let Owen watch the kids. I felt like I didn't deserve them. In fact, I was afraid Child Welfare would come and do an investigation. Maybe take them away." Janie stopped, aware that she had maybe said too much. "I'm sorry. I don't know why I'm dumping all this on you. You barely know me or my kids."

"I know you and your kids well enough, and I'm glad you told me." Luke gave her a crooked smile. "I don't think you'd ever have to worry about Child Welfare knocking on your door. You're a great mother, and you've got amazing kids." Then, to her surprise, he reached over and placed his hand on her shoulder. It was just a light caress, a casual assurance that he understood. That he didn't care.

But she felt a frisson of awareness as she felt the weight of his hand on her shoulder. A man's touch.

She gently drew back, and he removed his hand but his touch had created an imperceptible shift in the atmosphere. A heightening of awareness.

"Anyhow," she continued, trying to brush away the feelings, "Autumn seems to be much better. When I tucked her in tonight, she was asking about Cooper. She said she was glad he could run around the yard now that the new fence was up."

"I had to sneak some time away from the house to finish it, but I think it was worth it. I feel better for your kids, too. That other fence wasn't safe at all."

Now would be a good time to ask about the cost, she reminded herself, but she pushed the thought away. Later she would bring it up. Later she would find out what she owed him.

For now she could only afford to pay him for the flowers. But still she ignored the bills crinkling in her pocket and petted Cooper on the head, stroking his silky ears.

"So who's watching your kids now?" Luke asked.

"Dodie. She comes by once in awhile to help me with the kids."

"And so does your mom?"

"Not as often," Janie said with a smile. "I love her dearly, but things go better if we set clear boundaries."

"She's a good mother, though."

Janie caught the hint of melancholy. She shouldn't pry. This was none of her business, but at the same time she felt sorry for him. He was alone in this house, with only his dog for company. He lived in a small trailer parked on the yard. As far as she knew, he didn't know anyone in town other than the men who worked on his crew.

"Yes. She is." Janie scratched Cooper's head while she tried to find the way to formulate her next sentence. "I take it you don't feel the same way about your mother?"

Luke gave a short laugh. "My mother and your mother don't even compare."

"Why not?" She was fairly sure she knew the answer, but she couldn't seem to stop her mild prying.

Luke leaned forward, and Cooper turned to him, laying his head on the dusty knees of Luke's jeans. "There was a reason I was in a foster home."

He sounded so hard. Even his expression grew more grim.

Janie didn't say anything, sensing she would hear more if she simply waited.

"I don't remember her ever being there when I got home from school. Lots of times she didn't show up for a couple of days."

"How old were you when you ended up there?"

"I spent twelve years with my mom and then finally Child Services and the courts both realized she wasn't going to change, and I was placed in Al's home."

"What was he like?"

"He was a good man. My life got better when I moved there. He made me feel like a son. He and his brother Chuck were a real family to me." Luke's expression softened, and Janie wondered what it had been like for him at his mother's.

"Was he single?"

"Yes. Never married. He passed away a few years ago."

"I'm sorry to hear that."

"Well, you didn't know him." Luke angled her a gentle smile. "But thanks for that. Anyway, he was a good antidote to the times I spent alone, wondering if my mom was going to come back from the bar, from the party she had headed out to. Wondering if she was going to be around when I got up in the morning." He gave a short laugh, as if trying to diminish the memories with humor, but Janie caught the bitterness in his voice.

"I can't imagine what that must have been like." She wished she could come up with the right words.

And again their eyes met and Luke's expression softened. "You don't need to. It's over. I just wish my mother would clue in."

"Do you think she might want to make things right?" she asked, thinking about the phone call she had overheard earlier.

"I don't know how she could."

"Could she be looking for forgiveness?"

Luke looked away, his jaw set in a tight line. Janie felt the clumsiness of her words, as if she had stumbled into a place she had no right to be.

"I'm sorry," she said. "I had no right."

Luke waved off her apology. "Doesn't matter. Though I appreciate the concern." He stroked Cooper's head, Cooper barked and the moment was broken. "Do you want some tea or juice or something?" He waved his hand around the house. "I'm not exactly set up for entertaining, but I can get you something from the trailer."

"No, thanks. I should get back to the house and the kids." It was time to finish this so she got up and pulled the money out of her pocket.

Luke frowned. "*Now* what are you trying to pay me for?"

"The flowers."

Luke pressed his hands on his knees, pushing himself to his feet as he shook his head. "Cooper wrecked those plants. I am the one who is obligated to pay."

"But you bought more expensive plants."

"I bought what I thought was a suitable replacement. So put your money back into your pocket. I'm not going to take it." He softened the anger that had crept into his voice with a smile.

Janie felt a little foolish, standing across from him with her hand held out. How long should she wait?

"Would you consider it a down payment on the fence?"

"You're not paying for the fence, Janie. So put those bills back in your pocket right now."

"But—"

"To quote Robert Frost, 'Good fences make good neighbors.'" Luke laughed. "And don't look so surprised. I don't just read blueprints and the instruction manuals that come with tools."

"I didn't think that," Janie protested.

"Well, I like the poem. It fits."

"Why?" She knew the answer but was curious to hear what he would say.

"Your inability to grasp the application requires that one delves into the full meaning of the poem. To understand that in our situation, a good fence is a prerequisite for harmonious relationships." He grinned. "See? Not so dumb after all."

Janie caught a hint of mischief. "Not so dumb, but I think I can top that."

"Oh, do you read, too?" His question held a tone of challenge mixed with humor.

Janie thought a moment. "You do realize that in the poem, Robert Frost was mocking his stodgy neighbor and his propensity to create boundaries that delineate lives." Janie let a teasing note enter her voice. "He mocks his neighbor's desire for conformity and his repeated digression into proverbs handed down from father to son."

Luke looked impressed. "Got me beat. I'm guessing you took English lit in college."

"Immersed myself in one year of it."

"And then?"

And then Suzie came. "I changed my mind and quit."

"And eventually opened a coffee shop?"

"That was done out of necessity." Janie stopped there. She had already told this man too much. Had talked to him too long. If she stayed any longer, she'd be spilling all her dark thoughts, secrets and guilt.

She didn't want to give anyone that hold over her, especially not a man she barely knew.

"Anyhow, thanks for the offer of something to drink." She tucked her money back in her pocket. "We'll talk about that fence another time."

"Yeah. Just like real neighbors. Across a fence I just built."

They shared a smile that birthed a peculiar feeling, a connection she had never felt before.

She dragged her gaze away as her heart shifted into new and unsettling territory.

As Janie walked through the gathering dusk toward her home, she felt as if the boundary she had striven so hard to maintain between her family and the outside world had been pushed on and had wobbled. Ever so slightly.

In those few moments in the house, she had shown him more of herself than she had shown Owen in their whole marriage.

Danger, Janie Corbett. Big danger.

The words pealed through her mind as she walked up the front walk toward her house, each step toward her children reminding her of the necessity to keep Luke at arm's length.

Chapter Six

"**S**uzie, have you seen the magazine Grandma lent me?"

Janie flipped through the orderly stack of papers in the magazine rack. A couple of months ago, while they were having dinner at her parents' place, her mother had handed her a magazine. The cover promised ten ways to keep your marriage healthy, five ways to keep your garden flourishing and seven things a single mother should know.

It also held a recipe that Tilly had suddenly decided she needed. Immediately. Could Janie bring it when she dropped the kids off before Janie's mysterious meeting?

Janie had suspected the recipe request had a dual purpose. One was code for "did you read the magazine?" Which she hadn't. The other was an underhanded way of finding out more about Janie's appointment with her banker.

"Suzie. Did you hear me?" Janie glanced back at her daughter, curled up in one corner of the couch engrossed in the geography magazine Tilly had bought for her. Well, surprise, surprise. Janie hadn't thought Suzie would even give the magazine a second look.

Suzie glanced up, looking guilty. "Sorry. I was reading."

"I'm looking for the magazine Grandma Westerveld gave me a while ago. Has a picture of a couple on the front." A perfect couple with a perfect marriage because they knew the ten secret ways to keep it all together. And they probably never had to go to their banker with a creative expansion scheme designed to keep the business going.

"I don't know where it is."

"I need to find it, and then you make sure you're ready to go in…" she glanced at the clock. Three forty-five. "Five minutes." Part of her mind told her to forget it, but the other part, the part insisting she do this one extra thing and thereby prove to her mother that her life was indeed under control, sent her to the back room to the recycle box.

No magazine there either. She didn't have time to go looking, so her only other option was to show up empty-handed at her mother's place.

Melody, her usual babysitter, had a big date tonight so she couldn't come to take care of the kids. Dodie wasn't answering her cell phone, and Janie suspected her sister knew why she was calling.

This meant Janie was forced to call her mother to ask if she could bring the kids over. Her mother's moment of hesitation before she replied piled more guilt on Janie's shoulders, but she had no choice.

Janie had to close down the coffee shop early, as well. Which meant she missed the after-work rush, which meant she missed a surge of cash.

Once again she felt the weight of her responsibilities pushing her shoulders down, tensing her neck. Too much, she thought, dread scrabbling at the edges of her self-control. She couldn't do this anymore.

She shook her head as if to dislodge the thoughts.

There was no couldn't. She had no option. This was not her choice—this was her life. All she could do was pray for strength to get through each day. Each minute. She strode back to the living room to get the kids gathered.

But Suzie wasn't on the couch anymore.

The magazine she'd been reading lay tucked between the cushions of the couch. Janie bent over to pull it out and another magazine slid out from between the pages.

A teen magazine. A dubious teen magazine.

Janie's cheeks flushed as she read the semi-lurid headlines full of innuendo and promises of tell-all stories inside. What was happening to her sweet and innocent daughter? She had never worn lipstick or talked about boys, and now, within the space of what seemed like mere minutes, was loading up her untouched mind with this trash?

And where was Suzie now?

Janie saw a movement outside.

Suzie and Todd were on their knees at the end of the sidewalk, petting Luke's dog, who was straining at his leash, licking first Todd then Suzie. Her children were laughing.

Luke was wearing his jeans again and an old sweatshirt with a hole in the elbow, which made her wonder if the guy owned any decent clothes.

And yet he exuded an earthy appeal. Janie sighed at her reaction. Always did like those edgy guys.

As the words slithered into her mind, a harsh but realistic reminder of past mistakes, she pulled herself back to the here and now.

And in the here and now, Todd was supposed to be watching Autumn while Janie got her papers together for this very important meeting. If he was outside, where was his little sister?

"Autumn," Janie called out, wondering if her daughter had overcome her fear enough to be out with the kids.

"I'm here, Mommy," Autumn's muffled voice called out from upstairs.

Janie ran up the stairs, flung open the door and her heart fell. Her sweet adorable daughter, wearing the sweet adorable pink pants and frilly white shirt Tilly Westerveld had bought at some ridiculously high-priced shop, sat in the middle of Todd's floor happily playing with the felt pens she was never supposed to touch.

Her pants, her shirt and the floor around her were a storm of neon color, mocking Janie's sense of control.

"I made a pitcher," Autumn said, pointing with the bright orange marker clutched in her hand to the paper holding less color than Autumn.

No time. No time.

The words sang through her mind as she bit back the automatic reprimand and took the marker away.

"That's really nice, honey, but we have to get going." Janie forced a smile as she glanced at the picture. "Grandma is waiting." She flew to the room Autumn shared with Suzie, shoved open the closet door and flipped through the hangers looking for the other shirt her mother had bought for Autumn.

Nowhere to be found. Maybe in the laundry room.

She swung her protesting daughter onto her hip. Autumn was getting too big to carry, but time ruled out coercing her to walk faster.

"I want to go down," Autumn said, shifting on her hip. "I'm a big girl."

"Hold still, Autumn," Janie said, trying to catch her daughter and her balance.

But she missed the next step, and as she tumbled the rest of the way down the stairs, she heard Cooper's bark.

"He doesn't sit too still, does he?" Todd tried to pat the squirming dog's head.

"He's only a year and a half," Luke said. This would be mature for most other dogs, but labs were notorious for being late bloomers. "So you guys are all dressed up. Where are you going?"

Todd glanced down at his neatly pressed khakis, then jumped to his feet. "Uh-oh. My knees are dirty. Mom is gonna be mad."

"We're going to my Grandma and Grandpa's," Suzie said as she caught Cooper by the head and tried to make him look at her. "Mom has to go see someone at the bank." Suzie sounded bored with the whole proceeding and was far more interested in Cooper. "Can I hold his leash?"

"No. I don't want him to get away again."

"Please. I love dogs." Suzie's expression held that mixture of pathos and entreaty young teenage girls could pull together in the blink of an eye.

"Okay. But just for a few seconds. I don't trust him."

"He'll be fine," Suzie assured him.

"How has Autumn been?"

"I think she's still a little bit scared," Suzie remarked. "But she'll get over it. Mom was real glad you brought Cooper over like you did the other day."

"She was, was she?"

"Yeah. She always said since Dad's dog hurt Autumn, we'd never get a dog. But maybe if Autumn isn't scared, we might get a dog finally."

"So how long has your dad been gone?"

"He died a year and a half ago."

"I'm sorry to hear that."

Suzie shrugged as if brushing aside his sympathy. "He wasn't around lots before he died. Mom and him got divorced a long time ago."

"You're not supposed to talk about that stuff," Todd warned.

Suzie looked at Luke, then back at the house, as if wondering if her mother could hear.

"Maybe you should give me Cooper's leash." Luke said. Cooper was eyeing the front door of Janie's house, whining. Luke didn't want to destroy all the work he had done.

After Janie's visit the other night, he had kept his distance, chatting with Todd and occasionally Suzie over the fence he had built. Autumn still looked wary, but at least she laughed whenever Cooper put his head above the fence.

But come 6:00 p.m., closing time for the coffee shop, he kept his eye on the house, wondering if Janie would join the kids outside. Maybe give him a chance for some neighborly conversation. Over the fence.

"Everyone knows," Suzie retorted.

"Give me the leash," Luke said. He didn't trust Cooper's sudden interest in Janie's house.

"Mom doesn't like it when we talk about Dad," Todd said.

"And you're being a Goody Two-shoes," Suzie said, jerking a bit as Cooper tugged harder.

"Suzie. Leash. Now." Luke reached for the leash.

Her head jerked just as Cooper lunged. The leash slipped out of her hand and Cooper was off.

He got as far as the screen door, Luke right behind him. Cooper stopped, then barked, his deep bark reverberating through the house. Not again, Luke thought with dismay.

Luke caught Cooper's leash and pulled him away just as he heard a thump from inside, then a cry.

"That sounded like Mom," Suzie said.

"She sounds mad," Todd added, coming up the walk behind Luke.

Janie didn't sound mad. She sounded hurt.

Luke pushed open the door and ran into the house, Cooper right behind him.

Janie lay on the floor at the foot of the stairs, cradling Autumn. Janie's lips were white, her face pale and she was struggling to get to her feet.

Luke dropped to her side, pressing her shoulders down. "Stay there. Don't move."

"But Autumn…" She sucked in a breath.

"Is lying on top of you." Luke did a quick check of arms, legs. "And she's okay." He picked up the crying girl. Autumn screeched in his ear at the same time that he saw Cooper parked a few feet away, watching both of them with surprised interest.

"Get her upstairs," he said, handing Autumn to Suzie. "Now."

Suzie frowned at Luke. "Why?"

"The dog."

Suzie glanced at Cooper who, to Luke's immense surprise, still sat perfectly still, looking at Autumn, his head cocked to one side as if studying her. "I don't think she's scared of Cooper."

"Just take Autumn upstairs." He wasn't going to take any chances.

Thankfully Suzie took Autumn's hand and did what he told her.

"I gotta get up." Janie tried once more to sit up.

"Don't get up. You may have hurt your back."

Janie bit her lips as she closed her eyes. "My back doesn't hurt. My ankle does."

Luke did a quick check of arms and legs and then lifted the hem of her pants. "I'll need to take the boot off."

Janie struggled to sit up. "No. Just leave it alone. I have an important appointment."

"I don't think you'll be getting to any appointment." He was about to unzip the leather boot when she pushed his hands away.

"Don't. I have to get going."

Luke looked her in the eye. "You're not going anywhere."

She glared back at him.

In spite of her anger, in spite of the confusion of the moment, as their eyes met, something indescribable sparked between them.

And it wasn't just his wishful thinking. He could tell from the flush on her cheeks, the way she suddenly pulled away, that she had felt it, too.

"I have to go, Luke," she said quietly. "I'm meeting with my banker." Then her eyes glistened, and she pulled in a quick breath through her nose.

"Phone and tell him you can't make it. That you had an accident."

Janie pressed her hands to her face, as if holding back the emotions she had momentarily displayed. "I've rescheduled this appointment three times. He made a special effort to see me this afternoon. I closed the coffee shop early so I could meet with him." She took another breath, then lowered her hands. "Todd, get my purse from the table and that envelope underneath it."

Todd scooted down the hallway toward the kitchen.

"Thanks for your help. I'll be okay," Janie said.

"You're sitting on the floor."

"I'm getting up."

Luke had never met a more obstinate woman. "Let me help you."

She shook her head as she grabbed the newel post of the stairs and dragged herself to her feet.

A sudden cry escaped her lips, and as she wavered, Luke caught her. She tried to push him away, but he kept his hands on her arms.

"Okay. It hurts a little bit." She still held on to the post when she saw Cooper. "Where's Autumn?"

"Suzie took Autumn upstairs." Luke wanted to defend his dog, but Cooper shouldn't be in the house.

Then a thought chilled him. Had Cooper caused Janie's fall?

"Cooper, go out," he commanded.

Cooper didn't budge, looking vitally interested in what was happening.

"Go. Now," Luke repeated.

Receiving the same nonresponse.

"Cooper. Out. Now." Janie barked out the commands, and Cooper heaved a doggy sigh, got up and looked at Luke as if for confirmation.

"Now," Janie repeated.

And to Luke's surprise, Cooper trotted out the still-open front door.

"I've got to figure out how to imitate that 'mom voice' of yours," Luke said.

Janie tried once again to release herself from Luke's hold, her face twisted with pain.

"You're going to fall. Let me walk you to the couch."

"No, I can't sit around. I have to get going."

Luke gave her an oblique glance. "That mother voice might work on Cooper, but it won't work on me."

"Luke, I'm not kidding. I have to keep that appointment."

She started walking, heavily favoring her one foot, grimacing with every step. "Suzie, bring Autumn down," she called out. "Todd, give me my purse, please."

Luke wasn't getting anywhere with her. Despite her pain, she was leaving.

And he felt responsible.

"Okay. You're one stubborn woman. I'll take you."

"No. That's okay." Janie waved off his offer as she limped out the door.

Suzie came down the stairs, holding her sister on her hip. "So, what's going on?"

Luke sighed, then held his hand out to Todd. "Give me the keys, son. I'm driving."

Todd looked from his mother to Luke, unsure.

"And you're one stubborn guy," Janie said, sucking in a breath as she stumbled.

"You should know. Suzie, take your sister and brother to the car. I'm going to put Cooper in my house, and I'll be driving your mother to her appointment." He held his hand out to Todd, who gave him the keys.

Janie opened her mouth as if to nullify that but Luke dangled her keychain in front of her. "I'll meet you all at the car. Todd, could you please give your mother a hand?"

And before Janie could utter the protest he saw forming on her lips, he had caught Cooper by the collar and pulled him across the lawn to his house.

A few minutes later he was back at the car. Autumn already sat in her booster seat, Todd and Suzie sat beside her and Janie was easing herself into the driver's seat.

"Good try," Luke said, pulling on her arm and away from the car.

"You don't have to do this." Janie looked up at him with pleading eyes.

"Oh, yes I do," he countered, ignoring the look she gave him as he escorted her to the passenger door.

She was still protesting as he helped her into her seat, but he simply closed the door on her mutterings.

"So, which way is the bank?" he asked as he pushed the driver's seat back and clicked his seat belt on. His head brushed the roof. As he adjusted the rearview mirror, he jostled a yellow cardboard spruce tree he suspected was the cause of the coconut and pineapple scent in the car.

Janie twisted in her seat to check on the kids. "Are you all buckled in?"

"Of course, Mom," Suzie said. Did Luke imagine the slightly snippy tone in her voice?

"Suzie," Janie said, her mom-voice tinged with reprimand.

Luke couldn't help a quick glance in his rearview mirror. Suzie was sighing, but she didn't reply.

"Directions?" he reminded Janie.

"Sorry." She shifted again, clenching her teeth against the pain. "You should go to my mother's first to drop off the kids."

"And have her see you like this?" Luke guessed Janie wouldn't want her mother fussing over her. "I can take the kids to her place later. So, which bank?"

Janie bit her lip as she considered this. "I go to the one on Main Street. Down from the coffee shop. Todd, do you have my envelope?"

Luke turned, trying to make sure he didn't make any sudden jerks with the minuscule stick shift and tiny clutch. The one-ton trucks and eighteen-wheelers he'd driven seemed easier to maneuver than this itty-bitty car.

"What time do you have to be there?" Luke asked as he ground the gears, backed off and tried again.

"Two and a half minutes."

"That's shaving it pretty fine."

"I would have been okay if it wasn't for tripping down the stairs and finding Autumn…" She stopped and grabbed his arm, cutting off his little guilt trip over her comment about tripping. "Autumn. I can't let her go to my mother's like that. I was on my way to get a clean shirt when I tripped." She dropped her head against the headrest. "I'm doomed."

"I don't want to go to Grandma's." Suzie leaned forward taking advantage of the situation. "Why doesn't Luke take care of us?"

"Because" was her succinct reply.

Janie flipped open her cell phone and dialed a number. She tapped her one hand on her knee, shifted her feet and then winced.

"You should see a doctor about that, you know," Luke said. "What if it's broken?"

"It isn't…. Dodie. Finally. I need your help…you're at work? I thought the shop was closed. Okay, but I am really stuck." Janie glanced back at Autumn. "I can't take the kids to Mom's right now. Could you phone her and tell her I need to keep the kids at my house? Really? You're a dear. Could you meet me at the bank? Right away would be best… Great. I owe you. Thanks."

Janie snapped the phone shut, then turned to Luke.

"So Dodie will take over when she meets us at the bank. Also, she took her bike to work this morning, so she'll need a ride back to the house."

Luke knew it was the right thing to do, but to be honest he had been looking forward to spending some time with Janie's kids.

"Sure. Will do."

By the time they got to the bank, Dodie was sauntering down the sidewalk, her ruffled skirt swinging, her hair tied up in a neon-pink scarf. She looked as if she had scavenged the clothes from the thrift store she worked at.

Janie tucked the envelope into her purse and slipped it over her arm. "You kids listen to Dodie," she said. "And no television."

"Yes, Mom," Todd and Suzie replied, followed by a belated "Yes, Mom" from Autumn.

Luke turned off the car and hurried out, trying to get to Janie's door before she got out.

"I'll be fine," she insisted as he opened her door. "Just get my kids back home. I'll call my mother and tell her what's happening."

Luke ignored her protest as he tucked her arm in his and helped her up the curb. It felt good to be helping her. Felt better than good to have her arm tucked in his.

"What happened?" Dodie hurried over to her sister's side

"An accident on the stairs." Luke turned back to Janie. "What time should I come and get you?"

"Dodie can pick me up when I'm done."

"I can come and get you. That way she won't have to pack up the kids."

Janie waved away his offer, and Luke stifled his own annoyance with her.

Then she shifted her weight to her good foot, glancing upward. His annoyance drifted away as a soft smile shaped her lips. "Thanks for your help," she said quietly.

"Gladly given," he said, holding her gaze as a light spring breeze tossed her hair away from her face.

A glimmer of what they had shared before revisited, and

it was all Luke could do not to reach up and brush the errant strands of hair back into place.

Dodie was watching with avid interest, and Luke glanced away as Janie let go of Luke's arm. "Do you want me to start supper?" Dodie asked.

"I'll take care of that when I come home." Janie gave her sister a smile, Dodie gave her a hug and Luke felt it again. The faint touch of envy at the web of relationships surrounding this woman. Kids, sister, parents.

His mind slipped back to Al and Uncle Chuck. They had been generous and caring. His family. They had filled a void that his mother had created with her frequent absences.

But always, deep within him, was a deeper yearning for a family of his own.

Janie jerked open the door of the bank and hobbled inside. Luke waited to make sure she wouldn't keel over. An older man with thinning hair came out of an office, his hand held out in greeting. They chatted a moment, and then he was escorting her into a hallway. Just before Janie turned the corner, she glanced back over her shoulder.

Their eyes met again, and she ducked her head, as if embarrassed to have been caught, then disappeared.

"So, home again," Dodie said, a faint smirk on her face as if she had caught the little interchange.

Luke ignored the smirk and walked to the car. "Home again," he said.

Chapter Seven

"I understand the entire building that my shop is in is for sale. I currently lease half the building, so I was thinking of buying the whole building and expanding." Janie swallowed down the flutter of panic accompanying her brave words. Expand. So easy to say. It was the right thing to do. It was the only thing to do.

But second thoughts hounded her brave words as she handed Victor Chernowyk, her account manager, a folder with her proposal in it. The papers inside represented precious hours of work grabbed between working at the coffee shop and taking care of her house and children.

"I have a couple of proposals. One is expanding into the restaurant business, or adding a bookstore. I think the population of Riverbend could support a bookstore in conjunction with another business. Coffee shops and bookstores are a popular combination."

Victor opened her folder and flipped through the papers, his eyes flicking over them. He was only giving them a cursory glance.

"I've done a lot of research on those proposals," Janie said, a feeling of desperation coming over her at his seeming lack of interest. "I've gone through all the numbers…" Worn out her fingers on the calculator, contributed to global deforestation by going through reams of calculator paper. "Either of those could do well."

As Victor sighed and closed her folder, Janie swallowed down a bubble of trepidation.

"An audacious proposal, Janie, and one I'm sure your father would appreciate."

Janie gave him a careful smile, reading the undertone of his voice.

"The reality is, we've extended your credit as long as we possibly could," Victor Chernowyk said from his vantage point on the other side of the desk. "In fact, I've had to do some intense bargaining to get you your current extension."

And there it came. The dropping of the other shoe.

Victor smiled, the overhead light glinting off his glasses, his folded hands resting on the folder she had spent so much time on. "You're barely hanging on to your business as it is. Expansion is not an option. We've renegotiated the loan too many times."

Janie swallowed down the frustration building in hr chest. "So what is the solution?"

Mr. Chernowyk pursed his lips and leaned back in his chair, his hand still resting on her file. "Have you talked to your father?"

"That was never an option." Her words came out more forcefully than she had intended, but she needed to make this point crystal clear. "I'm not running to my dad every time I'm in trouble."

"Of course, I realize that," Mr. Chernowyk said, tapping his fingers on the file folder as if he were dealing with an obstinate young child.

And perhaps that's how he saw her, Janie thought, easing her foot into a less painful position. Victor Chernowyk had been her father's loan officer when Dan Westerveld first started his contracting business. He negotiated her father's first loan, mortgage and various other financing as his business grew and flourished.

Now Dan Westerveld's daughter was in financial straits, and Mr. Chernowyk couldn't seem to understand why Janie simply didn't go to the "Bank of Daddy" and take out a loan.

"I'm sure your father would want to know about your financial situation, however."

Janie couldn't disagree. She knew Dan Westerveld would willingly pull out his checkbook and fix it all.

After all, Owen would have asked. As the father of Dan and Tilly's grandchildren, Owen held a trump card that he played well and played often. He always managed to get money out of her dad as a result.

"He's not going to find out." Janie felt herself go cold and taut, and she sent a warning glance across the expanse of desk between her and her father's friend. "From me or you."

Mr. Chernowyk held up his hands in a gesture of defense. "Of course not. Our meetings are strictly confidential." He sniffed, then leaned forward again, his arms folded on the desk. "So that leaves you with one option. Selling the coffee shop while you still hold a small margin of equity in it."

"There's no other way?"

Victor sighed. "I'm sorry. Unless you find a partner who has the cash to get your operating loan in line, no."

And where was she going to find a partner? Her parents were out—and Dodie? Her flighty sister had a hard enough time holding on to a job, let alone partnering with her on a shop.

"I'll do some work on the numbers and see what I can come up with." Janie threw out the words as if they cost her nothing.

In which of your full twenty-four hours do you even hope to do that? And what numbers do you think will rescue your coffee shop? The file he's holding is full of numbers. What you need is money. Not more evenings hunched before a computer.

"What about the house?" She put this suggestion out as a last resort. She didn't want to jeopardize her home in her quest for independence, but if it helped, it was worth a try.

Victor shook his head. "I'm afraid the equity in the house isn't sufficient for a plan of this size."

Janie grew cold and taut as the exhaustion that had been her steady companion the past few years claimed her.

She'd taken over the coffee shop out of necessity. It had become her sole source of income and had, in the process, become a symbol of her independence from her parents. That she didn't need their help. That though marrying Owen had been a mistake, she was still in charge of her life.

"What kind of timeline am I looking at?" she asked.

Mr. Chernowyk blew out a sigh as he picked up a pen from the desk. "In about two months, interest on your current loan will reach critical mass."

And wasn't that a comforting concept.

"Thank you for taking the time to see me this evening," Janie said, slipping her papers into the envelope.

"No problem. Always glad to see you." Mr. Chernowyk stood as Janie painfully got her good foot under her, her hand resting heavily on the armrests of the chair. "Are you all right? You seem to be in pain."

His concern after his cavalier dismissal of her work, his easy assumption that she could run to daddy for help, got her back up.

"I'm fine," she snapped, though she was anything but. Her ankle throbbed with each heartbeat, sending waves of pain and heat up her leg but she managed to get upright without groaning or moaning.

"Of course." Mr. Chernowyk visibly pulled back, slipping his pen in the suit pocket of his coat. "I'll see you to the door."

He walked around the desk, leading the way out of the office. Janie followed him, stifling a cry of pain as she put her weight on her foot.

"You have hurt yourself," he exclaimed, frowning as she hobbled toward him.

"I twisted my ankle before I came here," she finally admitted. Fibbing about it further would only make her look even more foolish. "But I'll be okay."

"Are you sure?"

"Yes." Gracious, he was almost as stubborn as Luke.

"All right, then." He gave her another smile as he held open the door. He watched her go and then, thankfully, left.

Janie sank against the glass window of the bank, taking her weight off her foot. A few people passing said hello and she flashed a completely fake smile in return, hoping they wouldn't stop to talk. Between the pain in her ankle and the pressure building up in her head she wasn't sure what kind of conversation she could make.

From her vantage point in front of the bank she saw the pulled blinds and the Closed sign on the door of her coffee shop.

Which meant every person pausing at the door was one fewer customer and less income. All of which put the top of the hole she had been trying to climb out of since Owen had left her further out of reach.

For now, she had to get home and get supper ready for her family. As she pulled her cell out to call her sister, she felt a moment of panic wash over her.

Too many decisions. Too much to think about. And no way out.

"Cast all your anxiety on Him because He cares for you."

The Bible passage slipped in below the roiling of her mind, and she clung to it, needing the firm foundation of her faith in the shifting of her life.

Janie opened her phone to dial home. Then hesitated. Dodie would have to pack up all the kids to come here. Maybe she should phone her mother to pick her up and take her home.

And have her find out about the ankle, the shirt and the bank appointment?

She dialed home.

Suzie's "hello" was breathless, and in the background, Janie heard Todd laughing.

"Are you watching television?" Janie demanded.

"Luke is telling us stories."

"Why is Luke still there?"

"Auntie Dodie told him he could stay and help."

Didn't he have work to do on his house? Why was he spending time with her kids and her sister? Was he staying because of Dodie?

And why did she feel that faint tinge of jealousy? "Where is Auntie Dodie?"

"She's sitting right here."

"So Luke's been with you kids and Dodie the entire time?" she asked.

"Yeah. Luke made us clean up the house, and he's been trying to get Autumn's shirt clean. You can talk to him."

"No, honey, that's fine. Let me talk to Dodie."

But all she heard was some more giggling, then Luke's voice came on the phone. "I'm guessing you're done."

Her heart endured an unexpected pitch and roll at his deep

voice juxtaposed against the sound of her children's muted laughter. A man in her house, with her kids.

She decided to forego questions about his presence in her home. There would be time later. "Is Dodie there? I need a ride."

"Don't you think it might be better if I come get you? That way I'm not left alone with the kids."

She let his words sink in. "Sure. That would be good."

"I'll see you in a bit."

She wished she could tell him how she appreciated his consideration, his awareness of the precariousness of her situation. Instead she simply said goodbye and hung up.

She laid her head against the wall, her mind ticking back to a scene from the past. Owen was supposed to be watching the kids while she went grocery shopping. When she got home, she found he had left a note that he got a call from a guy at work and had to duck out. She didn't know when he got the call or how long he'd been gone, but when she got home Suzie was eating cereal in front of the television, Todd was stuck screaming in the bathroom, with a door he couldn't unlock and Autumn was playing with a pair of scissors.

She'd felt sick for weeks afterward, thinking what could have happened.

Her ankle was throbbing by the time Luke pulled up in front of the bank in her car.

Todd and Suzie had come with him.

What had Dodie been thinking, letting the kids come with Luke? She stifled her fear momentarily. They were here and they were fine.

She pushed herself away from the wall just as Luke got out to help her.

"I'll be okay," she said. But as she took her first step, an agonizing pain shot from her ankle up through her leg almost sending her to her knees.

Luke caught her and thankfully, didn't say anything as he escorted her to the car.

He helped her inside and waited for her to buckle up. "Luke hurt his leg, too," Todd said from the backseat. "He said he was in the hospital for two weeks. You won't have to go to the hospital, will you?"

"I can wiggle my toes. It's just a sprain." She ignored Luke's knowing look.

"Luke said he used to have a motorbike," Todd said. "Like Dad did."

"Hardly in the same class," Luke said with a vague smile. "At least guessing from the pictures I saw."

"The kids showed you pictures?"

"I thought it would be okay," Suzie said, picking up on the alarm in Janie's voice. "I wanted to show him how pretty you were in your wedding dress."

The thought of Luke looking at pictures of her past created a sense of connection she wasn't entirely comfortable with. And yet, as she caught his sidelong glance, the discomfort slipped away.

"I'm sure Luke doesn't care about my wedding," she said quietly.

"But he said—"

"And I'm sure your mom doesn't care what I said, Todd," Luke told him, glancing in the rearview mirror.

Thankfully he didn't look at her after he quieted Todd. Because in spite of her brave words, she tried not to wonder what he'd actually said.

The kids filled her in on the rest of the afternoon on the short trip back to the house. Apparently Luke hadn't had much luck washing the marker out of Autumn's shirt or the carpet upstairs. That he had tried made her smile.

"Thanks for picking me up," Janie said, slipping her purse over her shoulder as Luke parked the car. "And for helping Dodie with the kids."

Luke shrugged. "I enjoyed myself."

"And the house? Don't you need to work on it?"

"I got a fair bit done last night. I needed the break."

He sounded so matter of fact, and she didn't want to read too much into his comment or his presence.

The practical part of her knew she should be concerned about the kids becoming familiar with Luke. He was only temporary. But her mind was preoccupied with what the banker told her.

Tomorrow she could be the responsible mother and care-giver. Today she was tired, in pain and hanging by her very fingernails to the end of her rope.

"That's good." She gave him what she hoped was a polite smile, but as their eyes met, she felt it again. That familiar and dangerous frisson of awareness. That lightness of breath that was the precursor of longing.

She dragged her gaze and attention away and back to her responsibilities. Janie opened her car door and moved her foot. The pain increased by the minute. She didn't want to think what it would look or feel like once she took off her boot.

And then Luke was there, holding out his hand to help her out of the car.

She could ignore him, which would be foolish but rude, or she could put her hand in his, which would be danger-ous but smart.

His hand was warm, firm and as he helped her out of the car, his other hand caught her by the elbow, steadying her as she teetered on her single foot.

Suzie walked ahead of her; Todd was already on the step opening the door.

"Thanks for your help. I think I can make it to the house okay," she said.

She could tell he wasn't convinced when he put his arm around her waist and slipped her arm over his shoulder.

"Please, I'll be fine." But even as the words were formed and spoken, the lonely part of her yearned for the support and warmth of that strong arm around her waist, the feel of his broad shoulder under her arm.

Dodie was inside the front entrance when Luke opened the door, her cell phone in hand. "Great. You're back. I gotta run. Hannah needed some help with wedding invitations. She said she'd meet me up at her friend's place."

"Do you need a ride there?"

"Nah. Her friend lives only a couple blocks from here. I wish I could stay and help, but Cousin Ethan is pulling the 'left-out groom' schtick and wants to help with the invitations. Hannah is a bit worried, so I told her I'd run interference. Ethan usually listens to me."

"Yeah. Sure. Whatever." Janie felt a little disappointed that Dodie couldn't stay to help her out, but she had already prevailed on her sister's good graces enough.

Dodie gave her a quick hug. "You take good care of my sister, okay?" she said to Luke, fluttered her fingers at her nieces and nephew and then was gone.

"She's quite the ball of fire," Luke said as the door fell shut behind her.

"That's our Dodie. Always on the run. She's a great sister, though. A bit flighty, but a great sister."

Janie took a step, then faltered. Again Luke caught her.

"Where are you going?"

"Just get me to the couch," she said, her voice breathless at the pain and his nearness.

"So you have any pain reliever?" he asked as he led her out of the entrance into the living room.

"In the medicine cabinet upstairs."

"Todd, go upstairs and get your mother some Advil."

Luke helped her onto the couch and before she could stop him, gently unzipped her boot.

She couldn't stifle the cry of pain as he gently eased it off her foot.

"This looks just great," he said sarcastically. "You really twisted this."

Now free of the boot, the throbbing in her foot doubled.

"Do you have a tensor bandage?" he asked.

She shook her head.

"I think I've got one. I'll go get it."

"No," she said. "I'll be fine."

"You will not. You've got three kids who need you, and you can barely walk." Luke's voice was hard with anger as he stood. "Let me help you out. Besides, it was my dog that made you fall down the stairs."

"I'm not just being stupid about this, you know," she said quietly. "I've got to think about my kids. I can't afford to let you…" She stopped there, unsure of how to finish the sentence.

"To let me into your life. I got that. I'm just trying to help you. There's no strings attached."

But she knew the way she felt about him helping her up the walk and her initial attraction to him combined to weave a web she would have a hard time untangling.

"I'll be back," he said, and vanished before she could even formulate a response.

Chapter Eight

"No. You can't come over." Luke tried not to be taken in by the morose look on Cooper's face. "You've caused enough trouble." He tried to sound stern, the way Janie did, but he couldn't pull it off.

He bent and fondled his dog's ears. "You're a good dog. Just a bit of a problem from time to time."

He was about to leave when his phone rang. He would have ignored it, but it was the electrician he'd been trying to contact for the past couple of days. He kept the call as short as he dared, knowing Janie was probably doing exactly what he'd told her not to.

Janie wasn't on the couch when he stepped inside the house. Big surprise. The smell of onions frying lured him into the kitchen.

Janie stood by the stove, her foot resting on a chair.

"Are you nuts?" he asked, striding over to the stove. "I can't leave you alone for even a minute."

"My kids need to eat."

"And you need a bandage. Here." As he held it up, he made

a show of looking at her foot resting on the chair, her ankle now swollen and bruised. "You should put it on right away."

Janie's only response was a slight nod of her head.

Why did he bother? She didn't want his help. Nor did she want anything to do with him. He wasn't going to score any points with her.

"I'll just put the bandage on the table," he said.

Still no reply. But then she shifted to get something out of a cupboard over the stove. He saw her grimace in pain and, to his surprise, a shiny track of a tear sliding down her cheek.

The grimace he could ignore. The silence he got.

But the tear unmanned him.

He pried the fork from her hand and, taking a huge chance, clasped her around her shoulder, fitted his arm under her knees and lifted her off the floor.

"Please, put me down."

He ignored her even as her one arm clung to him and her free hand snaked up to wipe her damp cheeks.

"I have to make supper."

"I can help you with that."

"But you don't know my kitchen and you don't..."

"Stop, you're making me feel inadequate," he joked, ignoring her protests. He sensed she was simply going through the motions. As if not objecting was against an innate set of rules she had laid down for herself.

He settled her on an empty kitchen chair and pulled another one close with his foot.

"Do you have any frozen peas or corn?" he asked as he carefully laid her foot on the chair.

"I'm making chili for supper," she said, sniffing, still looking away.

Luke laughed at that. "I meant for your foot. You should ice it. Frozen peas or corn work great."

"I have some corn in the freezer up here."

Before he began digging, he turned the heat down under the onions. He found the corn, wrapped it in a tea towel and laid it on the kitchen table.

"Lift your foot," he ordered.

To his surprise, she didn't protest. He sat down, resting her foot on his lap, and began wrapping. Her ankle was warm, and she winced as he snugged up the tensor. "Let me know if it's too tight," he said.

"It's okay." She was quiet, almost reserved as he worked. Upstairs he could hear the muted sounds of Autumn singing to herself and Todd talking to Suzie.

The scent of sautéing onions sizzling gently in the frying pan, the onset of dusk. A woman sitting across from him, staring at his hands in the gathering quiet.

Possibilities and yearnings rose within his heart. He'd known since he was thirteen, what he wanted.

A home. A family. Al, his foster father, had given him that kind of life for the few years he was with him. He had hoped he and Jocelyn could share this.

Now he was thirty-five and staring at middle age, still single. And he was holding the ankle of a woman who was slowly, unwittingly, shifting into the emptiness of his life.

"That feels good," she said, her voice softly breaking the silence.

He put the final few wraps on it, tacked the end of the bandage down and placed her ankle on the wrapped corn. "That might not feel so good, but it will help," Luke said, standing up. "So. Supper. Why don't you direct?"

"I was going to make biscuits with the chili, but—"

"Which kind? Baking powder, cheese, yogurt, herb, sweet…"

"Are you kidding me? I have one biscuit recipe."

"You don't know what you're missing. Guess I'll have to see what I can throw together." He hoped he hadn't imagined the surprise on her face. He liked cooking and baking, but didn't get to do it often enough. "Okay. Onions are cooking. We need peppers." He glanced over his shoulder. "Texas chili or regular chili?"

"What do you mean?"

"Beans or no beans?"

"Definitely beans. Helps spread the meat farther."

"Okay. Beans it is." He opened the refrigerator and had to blink. Everything inside was in containers, labeled and organized.

"Peppers are in the—"

"—vegetable drawer filed under *P*," he said pulling open said drawer. "I should have known."

He heard a door open, Suzie yelling and Todd laughing. "What are those kids doing?"

"Hopefully, playing." Janie shifted in her seat and her face scrunched up in pain.

"Well, if that's all they're doing…" He walked to the bottom of the stairs and called out. "Suzie, Todd, come downstairs. I need your help."

"Oh, don't do that," Janie said. "They'll just get in the way and make a mess."

"So you'd sooner be alone with me?" Luke lifted his eyebrows.

Janie's mouth opened, then shut again, and she looked away, her cheeks flushed.

A hopeful sign, Luke thought. He called up the stairs again.

Todd showed up first. "What do you want me to do?"

"Get Suzie and Autumn down here. I need help cooking."

And in less than ten seconds he had three expectant faces looking up at him as if awaiting further instructions.

Okay. At least they *looked* willing.

"Todd, you go get some canned beans from wherever your mom keeps them, and then find a can opener. Suzie, you can start cutting up those peppers."

"She should put on an apron, Luke," Janie said from her chair.

"I'll be okay, Mom."

"And make sure you don't turn the heat under the pan too high. Otherwise the grease will splatter on the stove."

"What can I do?" Autumn asked, tugging on Luke's shirt.

Luke looked from Suzie, happily chopping and slicing, to Todd who was pulling out various cans from the cupboard, to Janie who looked ready to give more instructions.

He knelt in front of Autumn, pleased that she wasn't afraid of him anymore. "I think you can help me move your mommy to the living room so she can rest."

"No, that's fine," Janie protested.

"You hold your mommy's hand while I help her up." Luke pushed himself up, walked over to Janie's side, hooked her arm around his shoulder and slipped his other arm around her waist.

"I should stay here," Janie sputtered. "I should supervise. The kids won't listen to you."

"You should relax." Luke ignored her objections.

"But Luke. The mess…" Janie's protest died as Luke shot her a warning look.

"I'll clean up," he said with a tone that—he hoped—conveyed his complete confidence in his ability to do just that. "Autumn, you keep holding your mommy's hand so she doesn't feel afraid."

"Okay." Autumn looked up at her mother, as if to reassure her. "You'll be okay, Mommy, won't you?"

Janie shot Luke an annoyed look. "I'll be fine, sweetie."

As Luke walked her to the living room, he felt dismayed at the irony of this situation. He had this appealing and attractive woman in his arms, but it was against her will.

"So, Autumn, you find your mommy a good magazine for her to read. She needs you to be her feet for the moment," Luke said as he settled Janie on the couch. He gently lifted her foot and placed it on a pillow. "Comfy?"

"Oh, very." She sighed as she settled back. "You had a reason for this, didn't you? You want me out of the kitchen."

Luke pressed a hand to his chest. "You read too much into my simple actions."

"I'm sure." Janie glanced over at Autumn, who was rooting in the magazine rack. "Honey. Don't make a mess. Just get me the first one you find."

"But Luke said I had to get you a good magazine."

Luke didn't stop his smug grin. "See how well she listens?"

Janie rolled her eyes, and Luke couldn't stop the grin tugging at his mouth.

"Just make sure you clean up," she warned.

He saluted. "I'm a man of my word."

"Then you're a rare man indeed."

Luke wanted to stick around to find out what she meant by that. Wanted to know if it had anything to do with the man in the photo album—her husband, who was noticeably absent from the rest of the pictures. Her husband who had left her, according to the kids, well before he had died.

"So. Biscuit recipe?"

"In the red binder. Under muffins. Probably the fourth page in."

"Very impressive."

"And the chili recipe is—"

Luke held up his hand to stop her. "Chili is an entity unto itself. One should never follow a recipe."

Janie frowned. "How do you know it will turn out?"

"That's the fun of cooking. The surprise. The adventure."

Janie sighed and took the magazine, which Autumn had now found for her. "I don't think I want to know."

"Just the way I like it."

And he returned to the kitchen.

Should I be angry? Janie dropped her head back on the pillow as she heard giggling coming from the kitchen.

Autumn had stayed with her for a few moments but then wandered back into the kitchen. Janie didn't blame her. She wasn't much for company right now. She couldn't even read the magazine Autumn had so carefully chosen for her.

The events of the day roiled in her mind as Janie tried to decide what she could do.

Trouble was, the knotty lengths of her financial problem eluded her. And a man worked in her kitchen making supper and making her children laugh.

The sound sent a shot of pain through her heart. Since Suzie had turned twelve, she'd been fighting Janie on clothes, on schoolwork, going to church—just about anything that required Suzie to do what Janie wanted her to.

Janie hadn't heard Suzie laugh in months. And now, this man who had invaded their home was the one to elicit that elusive response.

She flipped listlessly through the magazine, then shifted the defrosting bag of corn on her ankle.

A bowl fell to the floor followed by a groan.

Janie couldn't stand it anymore. She reached over, took the bag of corn off her foot and made her slow way to the doorway of the kitchen.

"Wipe that up quick, before Mom sees it," Todd whispered just as she reached for the doorjamb.

"I'll need the vacuum cleaner," Suzie shot back.

Don't go inside, a quiet voice teased as she lingered between the living room and the kitchen, her ankle throbbing. Let them figure it out. Go lie down.

But if I don't go in there, I'll have more work to do later on.

She took a shuffling step forward, stopped and stared.

A cutting board sat on the counter covered with peppers in various states of dismemberment. A large bag of flour had fallen sideways on the floor and a trail of flour was strewn from the cupboard to the back door. Luke stood at the stove, barking out directions. Suzie and Todd scurried about, laughing as they tried to sweep it up, but only succeeded in creating a cloud of flour dust.

Janie could tell the second Suzie looked up.

Her smile faded, Todd glanced back and his hands fell. Only Autumn didn't notice. She knelt on the floor merrily sweeping the flour into a pile with her hands.

"Hey. What's up guys? Why are you stopping?" Then Luke glanced over his shoulder and frowned. "I thought I told you to stay put."

"What is going on?"

"An accident." Luke pointed a metal fork toward her. "Go back and read your magazine."

Janie hobbled into the kitchen, ignoring the shooting pains in her ankle. "You can't wipe up flour with a wet cloth, Todd," she said. "You'll turn it into glue. Suzie, you've got the wrong broom."

"And you've got the wrong idea." Luke put the fork down and walked over to her. "You aren't supposed to be here."

Janie had to tilt her head back to look at him. He was taller than Owen. Broader than Owen, and for a heartbeat, she felt a slither of fear.

"Janie. Please. Go sit down." Luke's quiet voice and his unexpected "please" combined with the tomato sauce on his shirt and the flour on his pants made the fear slip away. Owen never said "please." Owen never worked in the kitchen, much less spent time with the children.

And then he smiled, and her heart skipped again.

Janie pushed the reaction away as she looked at her kids, who were still watching her as if for further cleaning instructions. Until she had come and started barking orders, they were laughing and having fun.

And Luke had been the cause of that.

"It's okay to let go of control. For one evening," he said, tilting another smile her way.

Janie was suddenly bone weary, her shoulders slumping with the weight of her responsibilities.

"Okay. I'll leave," she said, spinning around. But she had misjudged her control over her balance.

Then she felt his hands on her waist, holding her up and supporting her.

Thankfully she was facing away from him, and he didn't see the flush warming her cheeks at his touch. Nor did he see the way her eyes shut as she fought the temptation to simply lean back against him and let him hold her up.

She had too many tangled and frayed threads in the fabric of her life. The only way to keep them together was to keep moving, keep tying off the ends and hope that someday it would all come together.

She pushed away from him and slowly made her way back to the couch, fighting the throbbing in her ankle. Once there, she picked up the magazine her mother had given her, sighed and turned to the article about the seven things a single mother should know.

Number one. Keep your children emotionally safe.

She'd thought she had that one covered until Luke and his dog entered their lives.

He's just helping, that's all, she reminded herself. Things just worked out the way they did. After tonight, he's back in his own house.

She turned her attention back to number two on the list. Take care of yourself.

Janie shook her head and skimmed over the usual advice about bubble baths and taking time off for the occasional manicure or to read a book.

Either the woman who wrote this was not a single mother or she was one of those high achievers who penciled relaxation time into her full agenda.

Janie threw the magazine down, closed her eyes and tried to ignore the noise from the kitchen and the slowly defrosting bag of corn lying on the living-room floor.

Chapter Nine

"Thanks for making dinner. It was really tasty." Janie smiled at her children, who were squirming with pride.

"Did you like the biscuits?" Todd asked. "Suzie made them."

"I used your recipe." Suzie gave her mother a shy smile, then glanced at Luke sitting across from Janie. "Luke helped me."

Though Janie kept her eyes on Suzie, she was fully aware of Luke sitting directly across from her. Having Luke working in the kitchen had been disturbing enough. Seeing him actually seated at the table, in the same place Owen would sit the few times he was home, created a tantalizing possibility…and served as a tangible reminder that men don't stick around.

"I measured the oil," Autumn added loudly, not willing to be outdone.

"And everything is just right," Janie said.

As she looked at the happy faces around the table, she wondered why she hadn't ever gotten the kids to help in the kitchen before.

Because you can't let go of control.

Luke's voice in her head annoyed her with its truth. She

had deliberately sat with her back to the kitchen counter so she couldn't see the mess. And she tried to ignore Luke, who seemed to be laughing at her, as if he knew exactly what was going on in her head.

"And you're not cleaning up," Todd announced as he started clearing the dishes from the table.

She caught Luke's warning glance. She could do this, she thought as she settled back in her chair.

"This is hard for you, isn't it?" Luke said with a cocky grin as Suzie, Autumn and Todd carried the dirty dishes from the counter to the table.

Her only answer was a vague shrug as she took a careful sip of the coffee Luke had poured for her. Everything would be fine. The kids were old enough to do the dishes.

A sudden crash behind her made her jump, and she twisted in her chair in time to see Suzie juggling a haphazardly stacked set of pots.

"Suzie, you should put the little one inside—"

"I think your mom and I will drink our coffee on the porch," Luke announced, pushing his chair back with a screech, which drowned out Janie's instructions.

"But the kids have never—"

Luke held up his finger to stop her. "Let's go," he said, taking her by the arm and helping her to her feet.

She wanted to protest but Luke didn't give her time. He escorted her through the living room, past the bag of defrosting corn, and helped her into a wooden chair.

"Okay. Foot up," he said, pulling a chair close. He ducked into the house and returned with a pillow from her couch in one hand, her cup of coffee in the other. Janie didn't even bother to object and obediently dropped her foot on the intricately embroidered pillow her mother had made for her. "Comfy?"

She nodded, cradling her mug in her hands as she forced herself to relax.

"I'm going to supervise the kids," he said, poking his thumb over his shoulder. "Are you going to be okay? Do you need anything else?"

"So now you're taking my needs into consideration?" She added a quick smile so he would know she was teasing.

He lifted his hands in a "what can I say" gesture.

"Go. I'll be fine," she said.

Which wasn't entirely true. She felt as if her life had taken a whirlwind detour and she was still trying to find her way back to normal.

You're okay. You're fine. Just let go. Enjoy the moment. Ignore the noises coming from the kitchen. You can fix whatever they broke or messed up later tonight.

Twenty minutes later, Luke towered over her, his hands shoved in the back pockets of jeans now spotted with water.

Janie didn't want to know how his pants got wet doing dishes. Later. She could deal with that later.

"So, that's done. The kids said they would get themselves ready for bed."

"Suzie has homework," Janie said.

"She's doing it. But I told her to help Autumn clean up her room first."

Janie had to lay her head back against the chair to get a better look at this puzzling man, still not sure where she should put him in her life.

He was a neighbor, but no neighbor had ever taken care of her children or cooked in her kitchen. In fact, her mother hadn't even done as much.

"Thanks so much, for everything." The polite words sounded inadequate, but she was afraid to tell him what she really thought.

That he was a great guy who was becoming enmeshed in her and her children's lives. That he was getting her kids to do things she never could. That her children seemed happier around him. Brighter.

More relaxed.

That he was awakening feelings in her with his consideration and his caring, which she had never thought would come to life again.

He scared her.

Luke squatted down, putting himself disturbingly closer to her. "You're welcome." His mouth tipped up in a lazy smile, creating appealing crinkles at the corners of his eyes. "But you might not be so thankful when you find out what I did."

"Washed my cast-iron frying pan with soap and water?" she asked in a breezy voice. She was alone with an attractive man, and humor helped to keep a distance between them.

He held up his hand, his face expressing horror. "Nothing so sacrilegious." He sighed, resting his hand on the arm of her chair. "I had to go and check on Cooper, and I ran out the back door and put my foot through your deck. I'm so sorry."

Janie waved off his concern. "I'm actually surprised that didn't happen sooner. Those boards were in rough shape when we bought the place."

"I'm coming back tomorrow to fix it."

"No. Please. You've done enough."

"I'll say," he said with a short laugh. "I made you sprain your ankle, and now I've wrecked your deck. But seriously, it has to be fixed. It's dangerous."

Janie felt the ominous weight of her financial situation settle on her shoulders. She couldn't afford to have him fix her deck. But she couldn't afford to leave it either.

"If you're worried about paying me, don't," Luke said as

if anticipating her protest. "I wrecked it, so I should fix it. I've got some leftover lumber we can't return to the store and I can't use on the house."

"I'll be fine."

"I'd hate to see your kids get hurt."

"Me, too. So I'll get someone to do it."

"Yes. Me," he pressed. "Besides, Todd and Suzie said they'd love to help." He smiled again, holding her gaze.

She looked away, recognizing that while she had allowed him to help tonight, she ran the danger of letting him creep too easily into their lives. "I'm sure they could. They don't seem to mind helping you." A tiny sliver of jealousy entered her voice as she deflected the conversation. She had never been able to eke that kind of cooperation out of Suzie.

"I guess it's because I give them space to help."

"More advice?" She blamed the edge creeping into her voice on her ankle, on the news she'd received only a few hours ago. And on the fact that she didn't know how she was going to run her coffee shop with a sprained ankle and limited mobility.

She didn't want to think it had anything to do with his nearness. With the way he was looking at her. Like she was even the tiniest bit appealing.

He shrugged, laying his hand on the arm of her chair to give himself balance. "I'm not trying to tell you how to raise your kids." His voice was quiet, a soft contrast to her ire.

She looked away, knowing she had overreacted. "I know. It's just as a single mom, everything I do is under extra scrutiny. If the kids mess up, there's an immediate assumption as to why. I don't want to elicit that reaction."

"You've got really nice kids. I don't think you need to worry about them messing up."

She let him cling to that illusion. It gave her hope that

maybe it could happen. Maybe Suzie would settle down and not buck her at every turn. Maybe Todd would come out of his shell at school. Maybe Autumn would stop dragging that bear around like a security blanket and talking to it as if it was real.

"I don't want to sound like I know it all," he continued. "I mean, I've never had kids, though I've always wanted to…" His voice trailed off, and he laughed lightly as if brushing his last comment away.

She took a chance and looked at him again. "How old are you, Luke?"

"Thirty-five."

"Ever been married?"

"Got close once." He scratched his cheek with one index finger, as if thinking. Remembering.

"What happened?"

"She didn't want kids." Luke's expression grew serious, and she felt drawn into his gaze.

"And you did," she said quietly.

He nodded, and as their gazes held, she felt the tiny beginnings of possibilities and potential. A single man who wanted kids. A single, attractive man who got along with her kids.

She shifted her hand ever so slightly until it touched his and his fingers curled over hers. His hand was large, rough and warm.

And then his face grew blurred. She didn't know who moved first but his lips brushed hers, a gentle touch, light as a butterfly, then again. And her soul, so long alone and lonely, teetered on the edge of longing.

She leaned forward as their lips met again, and he embraced her.

"Todd, get out of my room."

The screech from above them was like a douse of cold

water, and Janie jerked back. What was she thinking? Kissing this man on her porch while her kids were in the house?

"I'm sorry," she said, wishing her voice didn't sound so breathless as she tried to pull her hand away from his. "I shouldn't have done that."

"Why not?"

He didn't seem put out by her sudden withdrawal or her apology. Nor did he let go of her hand.

"My kids—"

"Are upstairs. They can't see us, and even if they did…" His shoulder lifted in a shrug that seemed to nullify her concerns and worries.

"They would get confused."

"They would think that I like you," Luke corrected as he looked down at their joined hands, his fingers lightly caressing hers. "And they would be right."

He spoke the words so easily that she almost missed their import. His presence, his persistence was wearing her down. Eroding her defenses.

"I can't do this."

"Do what? Talk to me? Spend time with me? What's wrong with that?"

She dug for all the arguments she knew she should have been using from the beginning. "My kids haven't had it easy with their father, and I can't afford to make the same mistake again. I have to protect them. To keep them safe. And Suzie…" She didn't bother finishing that thought. She and Suzie had a complex relationship. Introducing someone else into the mix would only make things more difficult.

"You don't think I'm safe?" he persisted.

Janie held his gaze as around them the sounds of the neighborhood settled into evening. "I don't know. I don't know much about you."

"So the only way you can find out more about me is to maybe make some room for me in your life."

"But to do that would mean I'm not putting my children first in my life. And right now I have issues to take care of. Resolve. To make room for you means I have to push something aside. And I have no idea what."

Luke released her hand and pushed himself to his feet. "I don't think you need to push something aside. I think you just need to let someone else take over a few things."

He made it sound so easy. So simple. As if all he had to do was slowly ease his way into their lives and ta-da. Instant family.

She had yearned for that, as well.

A complete family with a husband for her and a father to her children. But the path to that destination was strewn with so many potential pitfalls that to take even one step on that journey would open themselves up to a world of hurt.

"I've got three kids who need me," she said quietly, her attention on an elusive hangnail. "Three kids who depend on me to love them and to make sure their lives go on. Add me into the mix and we've got four bodies in this house. Four hearts with the potential to be hurt, bruised or broken." She dug down deeper, praying for the right words. "If you, let's say, date a woman with three kids and think she's the one for you and she drops you like a rock, you've only got your own broken heart to nourish and heal. But if I date a man who has no kids and he drops me like a rock, that's four hearts that need healing. I don't have the energy for that, Luke. And I don't want to expose my children to that."

The silence seemed to create a chasm, waiting to be breached.

"You're really thinking ahead."

Janie gave a short laugh. "I don't have the luxury of living for the moment like my sister does. I have to plan. I have to think. For the sake of my family."

"I understand that," Luke said. "And I respect that. In fact, I probably respect you even more for what you're saying."

She felt herself wavering, but pressed on. "And even more important is the faith issue."

"What issue?"

"Church. Faith. Dependency on God. First time around, I married a man to whom God was a swear word. He didn't come to church with me and the kids. I didn't have the support I needed to bring my children up as children of the Lord. My faith, my relationship to God is my first priority. Even more than my children." She kept her gaze fixed on something across the street.

"You don't know anything about my faith life." A defensive tone crept into Luke's voice. "You don't know what I believe or don't believe."

"I know you are aware of the commandment to keep the Sabbath day, but that only proves knowledge." She felt as if she was stumbling through unfamiliar territory with no discernible landmarks. But she also felt as if she had to press on. "But you're right. I don't know anything about your faith life. I don't know about your relationship with God, if there is one." She tried to gauge his reaction. "And that's part of my problem."

Luke sighed, then sat back, leaning against the house. "I used to go to church, if that's any help."

"Used to?"

"When Al, my foster father, died, I slipped away. Stopped going."

"Do you miss it?" She should have stopped, but even

though she had laid out the boundary between them—"good fences make good neighbors"—the lonely part of her who missed adult company, the female part of her who responded to his attention, kept her talking. Prying.

Hoping?

"Sometimes. But I keep myself so busy, I often forget which day Sunday is."

"There's a couple of churches in town here," she said. "Every Sunday, you've got options." It was his spiritual well-being she was concerned about now, she reasoned.

"I don't know if God would even recognize me if I came in, not with all the stuff I've done, or haven't done."

Janie chose to ignore that. She didn't want to delve into his past. "Of course He would," she assured him instead. "He says in Isaiah that He has engraved you in the palms of His hands. He is a loving and faithful father."

"I've always been thankful that Al could model at least that for me."

"Al was never married?"

Luke shook his head. "Nope. Though I had a brief moment of insanity when I thought he might marry my mother. As if Al would have anything to do with her."

Janie felt a moment of sympathy for the young Luke, lost, confused. Living with a man who wasn't his father, neglected by his mother.

No wonder he was looking for a family.

She stopped that thought right there. Luke didn't need her pity, nor did she have to harbor the faintest notion she could give him what he needed.

"You sound bitter."

"Yeah, well, my mom brings that out in me. Uncle Chuck keeps telling me to forgive and forget, but that's easier said than done." He stopped, then gave a short laugh. "Sorry. Over-sharing. That sounds bitter. I may not look it, but I guess I'm a bit of a dreamer. A happily-ever-after kind of guy. Not very manly of me, but there it is."

"It's a nice fantasy," she said. "I think all of us yearn for that."

"Did you?" Luke asked. "When you married Owen. Did you think he was your happily-ever-after?"

No, Janie thought. Never at any moment. Owen was the man her parents insisted she marry to make things right.

She'd tried to be a good wife. Thought if she worked hard enough, prayed hard enough things would work out. But they never did.

"He divorced me, remember," she said, the harsh word slicing through the soft night.

Luke nodded. "He didn't know what he was missing."

Luke pushed himself to his feet and looked down at Janie. "You're an amazing woman, Janie Corbett. You've raised three wonderful kids. You've created a life for them that any kid would be happy to have. And you did it on your own. You've got nothing to be ashamed of."

His words created a tantalizing image. A woman in charge of her life, family intact. The reality was so different. Secrets swirled beneath the facade.

He waited a moment, as if his declaration might break through her defenses. And it might have, if she'd allowed it.

"I'm sorry, Luke. I'm not who you think I am. I can't be that woman."

Luke ran his hands through his hair in a gesture of frustration. "I get it. I'm sorry I wasted your time."

Janie felt the sting of tears at the anger in his voice. As she watched him walk across the lawn, she almost called him back. Almost asked him to say those wonderful words again.

But then he jogged up the step of the half-finished house he was fixing up to sell.

He was dangerous and he was leaving.

And yet, as she slowly got to her feet, she replayed those words in her mind, "…amazing woman…wonderful kids… did it on your own."

"If only it were true," she whispered.

Chapter Ten

Janie gingerly worked her way across the porch and into the house. She stopped at the couch, picked up the bag of soggy corn and brought it to the kitchen, her ankle shooting pain up her leg at every shuffling step.

She turned a blind eye to the baked-on tomato sauce on the stove and the smears of flour still evident on the floor and counter. Later.

Autumn was already in her pajamas, standing on a footstool by the sink when Janie managed her way upstairs. Todd was squeezing toothpaste onto her toothbrush.

"Now make sure you get all the way to the back," he said as he handed his little sister the toothbrush.

Gracious, he sounded just like her, Janie thought as she braced herself in the doorway.

He looked up and grinned at her. "Luke told me we had to help you. So I thought I would help by getting Autumn ready for bed."

"Is Suzie in her room?"

Todd nodded, frowning as he watched his little sister

brushing her teeth with one hand, clutching her bear with the other. "All the way back. Just like Mom always does." He looked up at his mother. "I'm doing it right, aren't I, Mom?"

His look of worry and the concern in his voice was like an arrow to her heart. He sounded exactly like she did when she was younger, trying to make sure she did everything exactly the way her mother told her.

"You're doing just great," she assured him.

"Luke said we had to be extra helpful. Because you can't walk around as fast as you usually do." The little frown in his forehead deepened. "You're going to be okay, aren't you?"

"I'll be fine." She was a mother. It was her job to remove that worry line from his forehead. But the throbbing in her ankle gave the lie to her words.

Who takes care of a mom when she's hurt? she thought as self-pity hovered, waiting to move in. She quashed the emotion and soldiered on.

She walked with the kids to their bedroom, and as Autumn jumped into her bed, Todd pulled out his book.

"Can I read for a while?" he asked, sitting cross-legged on his bed.

"Just a little while. Autumn needs her sleep," Janie said as she eased herself onto the edge of Autumn's bed. She tucked the blankets as best as she could around Autumn and her ever-present bear, then stroked her hair back from her face. "So kids, tell me two good things and two bad things about today," Janie said, following their usual bedtime ritual.

"I have lots and lots of good things," Autumn said, her grin edged with toothpaste. "So does Berry Bear."

"Tell me two," Janie said, wiping the smear from her daughter's lip.

"I got to look at pictures. And I got to help set the table. And Berry Bear and I watched Cooper play with a Frisbee."

"We watched him over the fence," Todd added with a chuckle. "He likes to catch the Frisbee, but sometimes it hits him in the nose."

"And then he doesn't know where it went," Autumn said. "Berry Bear thought it was funny." Autumn turned to her bear, holding it up. "Didn't you think it was funny?"

"Like when Luke pretended to throw it and Cooper started running," Todd added, laughing at the memory.

Janie let them chat back and forth, letting their upbeat mood buoy her up, ignoring Autumn's constant interjections to her bear. In spite of the bigger age difference between Autumn and Todd, Todd was more connected to Autumn than to Suzie.

As was she.

She pushed down the errant thought.

"So let's say our prayers," Janie said as the conversation wound down. The pain in her ankle slowly increased as the painkiller she had taken wore off.

Todd put the book down, Autumn snuggled farther into her bed, her hands covering her eyes, and together they recited the prayer Janie had learned as a young girl at her mother's side.

"…and bless Todd and Mommy, and Grandma and Grandpa." Autumn opened her hands. "Can Berry Bear pray for Luke?" she whispered.

She wanted to say no, but what kind of lesson would that be? So she nodded her head. Autumn's hands held her bear's hands, she closed her eyes again and she took a deep breath. "And be with Luke. Thank You that he let us chop the peppers and thank You that he helped Mommy. Help that he can come babysit again. Amen."

From the mouths of children, Janie thought as she tucked the blankets up around Autumn's chin.

"I like Luke," Autumn said as she wrapped her arms around her bear, her simple words stirring up a swirl of unwelcome feelings.

What she had feared was happening. Luke was in her kids' lives. Luke, who was here temporarily and moving away as soon as he fixed up that house.

What would they think if they knew about that kiss downstairs?

"I'm glad you like him. It was nice of him to help us out," Janie agreed, renewing her resolve to maintain a distance from the man. "Have a good sleep." She kissed Autumn goodnight, patted Autumn's bear, then kissed Todd. He smiled as she stroked his hair back from his face.

Her precious children, she thought as a wave of maternal love swept over her so strong and intense it threatened to topple her. How she wished she could sweep all the barriers in their lives away. But she was only a mom.

"Love you," she whispered, kissing his little-boy cheek again. As she straightened, she wondered how long it would be before he stopped letting her.

She eased the door closed and leaned against it a minute, gathering up strength to walk across the hall to the bathroom.

She rummaged through the medicine cabinet and found another bottle, shook out the last two tablets and popped them down. One more thing to add to the growing grocery list.

On the way back to her bedroom, she paused at Suzie's door. The music from her room throbbed in time with her ankle.

Suzie sat on her bed, and as soon as the door opened, she slammed shut the book she was reading. Questions rose, waiting to be formed, but Janie let them drift down again.

She and Suzie shared a relationship that required a delicate balance of caring and discipline, and right now she didn't have the energy to negotiate her way through that particular matter.

"How much longer is your homework going to take?" Janie asked, raising her voice above the music pounding out of Suzie's stereo.

"Another half hour."

Janie hesitated in the doorway as she studied her oldest child. So like her father in many ways. And just like her father, Suzie often tested her at every turn. From the eighteen hours of labor to the four months of colic to the numerous ear infections, the first three years of Suzie's life were a litany of crying and headaches and questions about her mothering ability. Suzie grew up and things changed, but Janie always felt as if her daughter kept her at arm's length. As if she knew.

Janie shifted her weight as the pain in her ankle grew.

"Make sure you do your devotions, okay?" Janie asked, hoping and praying that Suzie would. It had been a few years since her daughter even let Janie participate in her evening prayers.

Suzie nodded, then gave Janie a look so much like her father she suffered a moment of frightening déjà vu.

Please, Lord, she prayed. *Don't let her turn out like her father. Please let her make good choices. Please don't make me pay her whole life for the mistakes I made at the beginning of her life.*

Janie held her steady gaze for a heartbeat longer, as if seeking some semblance of her family in Suzie, some hint of Westerveld to counteract the Corbett.

"Have a good sleep, Mom," Suzie said, her smile softening. "I hope your ankle is better in the morning."

"Thanks, honey. I love you."

Suzie simply nodded, her stock response to Janie's affectionate comment.

A few minutes later she eased herself into her own bed, gratefully taking the weight off her foot.

It was nine-thirty, her bedside clock informed her, as she slipped between the sheets and reached for her Bible. Usually she was doing laundry or washing the floor.

Which meant she would have to leave that work until her ankle was better, and who knew when that would be? And how was she supposed to run her coffee shop on a bad ankle? If she couldn't keep her coffee shop going, how in the world was she supposed to pay the bills that were slowly piling up? Make payments on a loan accruing interest as she lay there, her ankle pounding in time to the beating in her head. Pay her babysitter?

Don't panic. Don't panic.

Janie breathed her way through the fear spiraling up from her center. Get through this crisis one day and one step at a time. Like always.

She opened her Bible to the passage she'd read last. She'd made a promise to herself and God that she would work her way through the entire Bible this year, drawing strength and encouragement from every aspect of the Bible, no matter how obscure or boring it might be.

But the lists of rules and death sentences depressed her, and tonight she needed encouragement. She flipped through the New Testament her eyes skimming, seeking. She stopped at Colossians 3.

"Since, then, you have been raised with Christ, set your hearts on things above, where Christ is seated at the right hand of God. Set your minds on things above, not on earthly things." She paused a moment, letting the words take root, letting them fill her.

She was caught up in the things of this world. But what else could she do as a single mother of three dependent children? How could she balance her assurance in Christ that this world wasn't everything and yet be a faithful steward of what God had given her? Of her home, her business and, most importantly, her children?

The music across the hallway grew louder as did her annoyance.

"You're an amazing woman, Janie…"

Luke's words reverberated through her mind, intensifying her guilt. He saw only what he wanted to see. She knew he was slowly becoming a part of their lives. Her children prayed for him tonight.

She felt her heart falter, along with her resolve. She couldn't let him in. She couldn't open up a space for him.

He's already in. He's coming tomorrow to fix your porch.

Oh, Lord, she prayed, trying to refocus. *Help me to be the mother I should be to Suzie. Help me to love her as I should.*

The usual motherly guilt she felt over each of her children intensified as she prayed for her eldest daughter. From the day Janie found out she was pregnant with Suzie, her emotions had veered from guilt to anger over her predicament. She had kept her secret from her parents while she battled with her conscience.

For a time she had even considered running away to a place for unwed mothers so she could give the baby up.

Until her parents found out and shame and disgrace were added to her burdens.

So she did the dutiful thing: married Owen, had some happy years and had two more children.

But mostly she had her struggles. Owen was not father or husband material. Truth be told, she was secretly thankful he had left and then sued for divorce. Her life was hard now, but it had been harder when Owen was in her life, conveying the illusion of support.

He had never, in all the years they had been married, done even half of what Luke had done tonight.

Janie let her mind slip back to that moment on the porch as her fingers drifted to the lips Luke had kissed.

With a shake of her head, she tried to dislodge the memory, but the touch of his lips on hers, the feel of his arms supporting her was a tantalizing memory and a hint of what could be.

She slammed the door on that thought. Anything or anyone else would so completely disrupt her life, it would fall apart.

Besides, she had no right.

Please, Lord. Help me to find my completeness in You and in my children. They need me the most, and I need to be the best mother I can.

Chapter Eleven

"I vote Luke goes for the coffee run."

Luke dropped his hammer in his pouch and shot Dave a warning look. The last thing he wanted to do was head over to Janie's coffee shop and put himself into a potentially embarrassing situation.

But he could hardly explain that to a group of guys. His crash and burn of last night was seared into his memory.

You're an amazing woman.

He felt like smacking himself on the head. These were supposed to be the magic words that would break down her defenses? Prove to her that he was worth a second look?

Crazy. Clearly crazy and desperately out of practice.

For a moment he truly thought something was happening between them. Something he wanted to build on and, he foolishly thought, something she was willing to take a chance on.

Clearly, not.

"Bert can go," Luke said as he heaved a sheet of drywall into place. "I've got to finish this up."

"Oh, c'mon, you know that Dave's faster at nailing than

you." Bert picked up the jar holding the coffee money. "You may be the money guy, but I'm the foreman." He gave the jar a shake. "So. Go."

Luke relinquished his hold on the sheet to Bert and took the jar.

May as well go. He had finally finished the book he'd been reading the night before. Maybe he'd have a chance to pick something else up.

He drove down main street, looking for a parking spot when a car pulled out right in front of him.

And right in front of the coffee shop. A sign? Or simply the only empty spot on the street.

He pulled in, parked the truck and sat there a moment.

He'd been told fairly clearly what was going on in Janie's life. He'd been warned. He turned off his truck and sat there a moment while he tried to decide how he was going to play this.

Casual would be best. As if nothing had happened the night before.

While he made his plans, he glanced at the empty building beside Janie's. It looked as if it had been empty for awhile.

And it had a For Sale sign in the window. He wondered if Janie leased her half of the building or owned it. A quick phone call to the number below the For Sale sign would answer that question.

Cooper shifted his paws on the seat, emitting a nasal whine, as if urging Luke to do something.

This was a bad idea, Luke thought resting his hands on the steering wheel. You're going to look like you're desperate to see her again.

"Okay. Here goes nothing," he said to Cooper. "I got elected to do the coffee run, and this is the best place to get it, right?"

Luke adjusted his ball cap. He ran his hand over his cheeks. Raspy, but he wasn't about to primp for a coffee run.

Cooper jumped down from the seat, his expression expectant. "Sorry, mister. I'll only be awhile. You stay."

Luke pulled in a quick breath, stepped out of the truck, paused a moment, then decisively walked the other way. Best if he tried to find a book before he got the coffee, he reasoned.

Ten minutes later, he didn't find a place selling anything else than the top twenty bestsellers or magazines. Selling books was obviously not a priority in this town, but he didn't have time to go looking. If he wasted too much time in town, he'd run the risk of having grumpy workers. Grumpy workers were slow workers. The clock was ticking.

His wanderings had taken him back to the coffee shop, and with a sense of inevitability he walked past the vacant office beside the coffee shop.

As he neared the door, he glanced into a window of the shop facing the street and was surprised to see Janie sitting at a table. Talking to the banker. She was giving him some papers.

He wondered what that was all about as he pulled open the door and stepped inside.

He was greeted by the clink of cups, the buzz of dozens of early morning conversations. The place was hopping.

An unfamiliar girl stood behind the counter dispensing coffee. Long curly hair, the color of copper, pulled back in a ponytail and covered with the same kind of bandanna Janie always wore.

The girl looked up, smiling as Luke came near. "What will you have?"

Luke gave his order, reaching back to pull his wallet out of his pants. While he did, he glanced around surprised to see Janie's mother wiping down tables and gathering up coffee cups. His first impression of her wouldn't have placed her in this scene. His eyes flicked to Janie, who was getting up from the table, her expression even stonier than the one he got last night. She grabbed a pair of crutches and thumped toward the counter, moving right past him without even seeing him.

Or she could be ignoring him.

She made it around the counter before looking up and, as she did, her eyes met Luke's.

Her blush was a surprise.

"So you got help today," he said aiming for casual.

"My mom showed up this morning, and Hannah came later." Janie thumped over to the refrigerator and pulled out a jug of milk, setting it beside Hannah.

Hannah glanced from Luke to Janie, a spark of mischief in her eyes. "Janie, aren't you going to introduce us?"

Janie spun around, frowning. "Luke, this is Hannah. She's marrying my cousin, Ethan Westerveld. Hannah, Luke."

Her abrupt tone only served to underline the reasons he didn't want to come here. Enough with the humiliation already.

Hannah gave Luke a quick once-over. "So, how do you know our Janie?"

Before Luke could answer, Janie said, "He's rehabbing the house next door to mine." She hobbled back to the cash register. "So he can flip it."

Her words sounded hard, as if she had to say them out loud to convince herself. To push him away.

"I'm excited to see what you're going to do with it." Hannah flashed Luke a quick smile. "Do you do other carpentry work?"

Luke glanced at Janie and nodded. "From time to time."

Hannah's eyes brightened. "Great. My fiancé's house could use some work. Would you be able to do that?"

"I don't know for sure. I'd have to talk to my partner," Luke said, hesitating. His only deadline was getting this house done, and after that, he didn't have much reason to stick around.

He glanced at Janie who was now watching him. His mind ticked back to something she had said about him moving on. And he wondered if that was part of her shutting him out.

"I might be able to fit it in, though," he said.

Janie held his gaze for a heartbeat, then looked away. But in that glance, he caught a flicker of hope that gave him hope. "Hannah, I think Luke might want to order" was all she said.

"I'm getting his order now."

Luke's eyes were on Janie. While she helped Hannah mix the coffees, she glanced his way again. Hardly the actions of a completely disinterested party, he thought, hope nudging at the grumpy mood he had entered the shop with.

"You have good taste in coffee, Mr. Harris." Tilly walked around him and the counter, a faint challenge in her voice.

"Hello, Mrs. Westerveld," Luke said. "Nice to see you again."

Tilly gave him a tight smile, added a lifted eyebrow as if she didn't quite believe him, then turned to her daughter. "A couple of those sugar containers need to be replaced. The spouts don't work properly."

"Sure, Mom," Janie replied, turning to wipe down the counter in front of her. "I'll write that down."

Janie faced Luke, her back to Tilly so he caught the faint eye roll and the hint of a sigh in the lift of her shoulders.

"I cleaned out the back room, too. It was quite dirty."

Another eye roll.

"And you might want to look at a few of your chairs. They wobble. Add that to your list, too."

Janie's only reply to her mother's assertive comment was

a tight nod. She looked tired, and though he was certain her mother meant well, he guessed Janie simply didn't need the extra work right now.

"I can take a look at the chairs," Luke offered.

Tilly glanced at him, as if she had forgotten he was there.

"Just tell me which ones they are. I've got a few tools in the truck."

"Your coffees are ready," Hannah said, handing Luke a cardboard tray with four cups.

"They'll stay hot for a while."

Tilly gave Luke another once-over and then beckoned with her finger. "Very well. Follow me."

He wove around the tables with customers. A few people glanced up at him. Some smiled. The place was full. Obviously business was good.

"It's these two," Tilly said, giving the offending chairs a quick shake.

Luke tipped them over and figured out what the problem was. One quick trip to the truck and a few minutes later he had the screws holding the legs to the chair frames tightened. Checked out the table for good measure and had managed to tweak a smile out of Janie's mother.

"Thank you, Luke. We appreciate your help." Tilly's attitude had thawed a half a degree.

"Anytime." He sauntered over to the counter and picked up his order.

Janie frowned at him, glanced over her shoulder as if to make sure her mother was far enough away, then leaned forward. "What are you doing?" she whispered.

"Fixing your chairs," he whispered back.

Janie gave him with a warning look. "And that's all?"

"Looks like it."

"Okay." As she pulled back, he saw Hannah watching them. He tossed off a wave and left the shop, feeling pretty good about himself.

Chapter Twelve

In spite of the three Advil she took after work, Janie's ankle still throbbed. She knew she had worked too hard at the shop today, but she was determined to show her mother that it wasn't as bad as it seemed.

After that all she wanted was to come home, crawl into bed, pull the sheets over her head and shut out the world. Of course her mother wanted to know what her banker, Victor, and she had talked about, and of course, Janie didn't tell her.

Instead she had gone to the storage room, popped some Advil and soldiered on: working, pulling shots when she could, bantering with the customers and with Hannah. Then, just after supper, she had taken an extra dose of Advil, and as a result, her head was now buzzing from the pills.

"Suzie, can you get my mug from the living room?" she called out, suddenly remembering the cup she had left there when she had come home from work. Her mini vacation. Drinking tea for five minutes.

"I thought I was done helping." Suzie's petulant voice grated on Janie's already-fragile nerves. Why did she bother getting Suzie to help?

Because Luke was right—as much as it bothered her to admit it. She needed to get the kids to help more.

"Just do it, Suzie."

Suzie's sigh was out of proportion to the work she had to do, but Janie ignored it and thankfully Suzie headed to the living room.

Once again Janie's eyes flitted to the holiday trailer parked in the yard beside them. The lights were on. Luke must be finishing supper. When he was done, he would probably go work in the house as he usually did. And then what? Go to bed? Wake up and do it all over again?

And when he was finally done?

Janie's heart fluttered in her chest as her emotions veered from resolve to longing. She felt as if she hovered on the edge of a place that, once entered, she could never leave.

Smart. She was playing it smart.

Suzie's noisy return pulled her back to the here and now. She opened the dishwasher, put the cup in and then, to Janie's surprise, rinsed out the dishrag and wiped the counters.

"Thanks for doing that, honey," Janie said.

Suzie threw the rag in the sink, lingered a moment, then turned to her mom.

"Theresa Springfield is having a party in a couple of weeks. She asked me to go. Can I?"

"Birthday party?"

"Um, yeah." Suzie's hesitation and the way she wouldn't meet Janie's eyes sent warnings jangling like a bell choir through Janie's head. She highly doubted, knowing the little bit she did about Theresa and the Springfield clan in general, that the party would include cake and party hats and a benign game of pin the tail on the donkey.

"You hardly know Theresa. You just started hanging out the

past couple of months." Which was a couple of months too long. Janie suspected Theresa had much to do with the magazines Janie had found tucked under Suzie's mattress. She knew she had to confront her on that matter sooner or later.

"She's my friend, Mom."

"Then she'll understand when you tell her your mom said no. And for now, I'd like you to tidy the living room and sweep the front step." Janie rested her leg on the kitchen chair as she rinsed the dinner plate before putting it in the dishwasher.

Luke's comment about getting her kids to help had made her rethink her ongoing strategy with her children. She knew Suzie needed to take on more responsibility. As Autumn and Todd grew older, Janie would need help. Maybe there'd even be a day she would need her help in the coffee shop.

It won't be around by then.

Janie pushed that thought down hard and fast. She couldn't think about that today.

"I brought you your mug. I wiped the counters. Why are you making me work so hard?" Suzie shoved her hands into the pockets of her jeans, glaring at her mother. "I have homework to do."

"I'm just asking for some help. I can't do all that work myself." Janie bit back a sigh. She didn't remember Luke having this much trouble getting Suzie to pitch in. Of course Luke didn't have the built-in guilt buttons Janie had where Suzie was concerned. Buttons that Suzie was often unaware she pushed.

"I think Todd should help."

Patience, Lord. I could use some patience right now. "Todd is cleaning up Autumn's room."

"Why couldn't I clean up Autumn's room?" Suzie whined.

Janie purposely kept her gaze ahead, fighting to hold on to her temper. She couldn't get angry with Suzie. If she did, all the frustration of the past week, the past month, my goodness, the past few years, would all come raining down on her unsuspecting daughter's head.

"Please just do what I asked, Suzie."

Suzie's sigh was like a blast of chill air, but Janie didn't acknowledge it. Soon she heard Suzie's footsteps stomping up the stairs.

Janie turned on the dishwasher and gingerly made her way across the kitchen to the laundry room.

It took her a few minutes to shove the basket of wet laundry along the floor and out onto the deck. Every step, however, was fraught with anxiety. The deck board Luke had stepped through wasn't the only rotten one.

Fifteen minutes later, the clothes swung gently in the evening breeze and Janie collapsed onto a plastic chair, resting her ankle. She just needed a moment to catch her breath, corral her thoughts.

She had to get the kids in bed, make lunches for tomorrow, mend Suzie's dance outfit and pay some bills from her overdrawn checking account.

Dread clutched her midsection with icy fingers.

You can ask your father for help.

Janie shook her head as if to dislodge the pernicious voice. Owen had done that enough. She was never going to follow in her ex-husband's footsteps.

But her pride had a cost, and it seemed she was paying it now. She was running out of options.

Let it go. Leave it be.

A sigh sifted out of her as the thought took hold. So much could be resolved if she simply let go. Stopped fighting.

And then what? Find a job in Riverbend? Work for someone else?

How would she support her children? Keep her house? Dread washed over her at the thought of losing the coffee shop and moving into an apartment. She tried to find her footing, tried to find the positive, but the panic took over and, combined with the pain in her ankle, broke down her defenses.

She laid her head against the house.

I can't do this anymore, Lord, she prayed. *I simply can't. Please help me get through this.*

A cold wet nose pushed itself against her arm and Janie screamed, her prayer forgotten. She pulled back.

"How did you get out?" she said to Cooper, smiling in spite of her wavering emotions. "Does Luke know you're here?"

Cooper didn't move.

"Go on. Luke wants you back." Janie gave him a gentle push in the direction of the yard.

But Cooper just sat there. He emitted a thin whine, as if commiserating with her. Janie gave up and leaned back again, resting her hand on Cooper's neck.

She took a long, slow breath. Abdominal breathing. Was supposed to help her relax.

Instead, as she breathed, and stroked Cooper in time to her breaths, she felt sorrow thickening her throat. She swallowed. If she started crying now, she wouldn't stop.

"My life is falling apart," she said quietly, talking to the dog. "I had such good plans. But it's all coming apart as quickly as my deck. I'm in trouble with the bank, and I don't know if I can afford to stay in this house."

Cooper pushed his head onto her lap as she unburdened herself, telling him things she hadn't been willing or able to tell anyone else.

The dog snorted, as if he understood, and Janie gave in to an impulse and laid her head down on his. His head was silky and warm, and Janie felt the beginnings of a sob fill her throat. Cooper licked her hand, and a tear trickled down her cheek onto his head.

"What am I going to do?" Another tear followed, and as Janie reached up to wipe it away, she caught a movement below her.

She turned her head to see Luke standing on the ground beside her deck.

"Hi there," he said, his voice quiet. "I see you found my dog or, rather, he found you."

At the sound of Luke's voice, Cooper turned but didn't move.

Janie surreptitiously wiped the tears off her cheek. Had he heard what she said?

"What's the matter?" he asked, thankfully staying where he was.

The concern in his voice was almost her undoing. "Nothing. I'm fine."

"Really?" He took a step closer and sat on the edge of the deck. He pulled at one of the boards, loosening it easily. "Level with me, Janie. You don't have anyone coming to fix your deck, do you?"

He was persistent, she gave him that. "No, I don't," she admitted, realizing he would find out soon enough when no one showed up.

Luke sighed. "I did break it. I feel I should fix it."

"Anyone could have broken it."

"Well, I did." He wiggled the board. "And look. I did it again. And since you don't have anyone else to work on it and since I have this extra lumber, why won't you let me fix it? I'll come when the kids are in bed. They won't even know I'm here."

"They'll hear you."

And I'll know you're here. Doing things Owen would

never even consider doing. Being helpful and considerate. Worming your way into my life.

As you already have.

Luke was about to protest once more when Cooper lifted his head, emitted two sharp barks, then bounded toward the porch door.

"Well, well, well. There you two are." Dodie stuck her head out the door, the lilt in her voice full of innuendo.

"Luke was just leaving." Janie got to her feet.

"Are you sure you don't want to stay for a cup of tea, Luke? I just bought a new blend at a cute tea-seller at a Farmer's Market in Whitecourt."

"Luke doesn't drink tea," Janie said decisively.

"So what brings you here, Luke?" Dodie asked, ignoring her sister.

"He wants to fix Mommy's deck," Todd called out from the window above them. "And I want to help him."

Janie was flooded with a mixture of embarrassment and anger with her young son for eavesdropping. How long had he been listening?

"It needs fixing, that's for sure," Dodie said. "You want a hand?"

"No fair, Aunt Dodie. I want to help," Todd called out.

Dodie stepped out onto the lawn. "We can both help," she called out, looking up.

"That will be fun."

Janie glanced from Dodie to Luke, feeling as if she'd been shanghaied.

"I'll stop by tomorrow night," Luke said, interpreting her hesitation for approval.

Just then Todd joined them outside. "You'll let me help, won't you, Luke?"

The hopeful note in her son's voice got her. Luke had done what she couldn't. Gotten Todd out of his shell. Pulled Todd out of his world of books and reading that she had mistakenly assumed was a positive but which had, instead, been an escape.

"Of course I will." Luke kept his gaze on Janie as if seeking confirmation. "If it's okay with your mom."

It seemed she had no choice.

"That would be okay," she said quietly.

"Great. I'll be by tomorrow night. After supper."

"So you coming in for tea?" Dodie pressed.

"No. I don't want to overstay my welcome." Luke gave Janie a wry smile. Then he whistled for Cooper and, together, they left.

Dodie sighed. "He's one great guy, Janie. I can't see how you can just let him walk away."

Janie poked her sister, then inclined her head toward Todd, who was watching Cooper, but she was sure, listening to them.

"He's just next door" was all Janie would say.

"Good thing," Dodie replied.

"Todd, you should get back to your bedroom. I'll come up to tuck you in right away."

Todd waited a moment, watching Luke and Cooper; then he turned to Janie. "I'm glad he's coming back," he said, grinning. He trotted off, the picture of contentment.

"So, did Mom send you here, or are you here on your own?" Janie asked as the door shut behind him.

"Got bored with my own company. Thought I would see what's happening here." Dodie glanced over to Luke's yard, watching with Janie as the lights flicked on in his trailer. "And it's a good thing I came."

"I suppose I can thank you for that," Janie said wryly.

"You weren't going to let him help you, were you?"

Dodie asked, suddenly serious. "You would prefer to let this deck rot away?"

"I have my reasons," Janie said, disliking the prim note creeping into her voice.

"Dumb reasons," Dodie retorted. "He's a great guy, and he is great with the kids."

Dodie wasn't giving her new information. But things were never as cut-and-dried as her sister thought.

Luke held a fantasy view of her complex and messy life and given how he spoke of his mother, he had his own issues.

"Do you see that trailer on the yard? That's where Luke lives," she said with more force than necessary. "Do you see that house? Once he's fixed it up, he's selling it. He's moving on, Dodie. He's not sticking around. And he doesn't go to church. Doesn't share the same values I do. There's too much that doesn't fit or work." She caught her breath after her little speech, not liking the smile forming around Dodie's mouth.

"Are you trying to convince me or yourself?" Dodie raised her eyebrows in question. "Because I think you're scared that he's sneaking into your heart."

Janie felt Dodie's words battering at her defenses. She had to hold on. Had to shore them up. She had nothing to fall back on if he hurt her. Left her.

"And you're such an expert on relationships," she snapped, her words sharp and hard, deflating the hope that had shone in Dodie's face. "You've had so many boyfriends."

Dodie reared back, and even before she was finished speaking, Janie wished she could snatch her words back.

"I'm sorry, Dodie. I should never—"

"I've got to go." Dodie's voice was quiet. As she turned away, Janie felt like a traitor. She had struck out to defend herself and in the process had hurt her sister.

As Dodie left, Janie pressed her hands to her face. *Forgive me, Lord,* she prayed. *I'm turning into a miserable old woman, pushing everyone away. I don't want to be that woman, but I don't know what else to do.*

She waited a moment, gathering her thoughts.

But just before she shuffled into the house and back to her obligations, she shot one last look over her shoulder at Luke's trailer. The lights were on, and she wondered what he was doing in there. All alone.

Chapter Thirteen

"No one came to work on the house today?" Janie stood in the doorway, watching Luke and Todd as they pounded nails into the fresh, white boards that were part of her new deck.

Luke pounded another nail in and sat back on his feet. "The crew staged a revolt last night. Said they weren't going to work on weekends anymore. Slackers." Though he threw out the comment with a smile, he felt again the smolder of anger he'd experienced when Bert gave him the news.

Before he came, the crew was working at half capacity, yet he was paying them a full wage. He was still trying to make up for lost productivity during that time. They were at least a couple of days behind on the job. Though it was Saturday, Luke had worked all morning and afternoon, trying to get done what he could on his own. For a moment he had thought about not fixing this deck. Janie didn't want him around anyhow, but he had said he would come.

And if he didn't and something happened to the kids as a result, he would feel terrible.

So he had scarfed down a quick supper, then showed up here, ready to pound yet more nails.

"Will you get your house done on time?" she asked, still hanging around.

"Oh, ya." He waved off her concerns with a gloved hand. He didn't want her to know how behind he was. It would only give her another excuse to keep him away from her.

And her kids.

Todd was grinning as he pounded nails with one hand and held on to his hard hat with another.

Behind him, Autumn swung back and forth on the swing, her bear on her lap, singing a little tune in time to the squeaking of the swing set.

He had taken a chance and had taken Cooper along.

Thankfully he had been surprisingly quiet and now lay beside the deck, catching the early evening rays of the sun, his tail twitching. Suzie had made an appearance for a while, playing fetch with Cooper; then a phone call from a friend had summoned her into the house.

Janie put her head out the door from time to time, answering questions he had about her preferences and, sometimes, just watching.

The watching part gave him a mixture of hope and encouragement. She didn't need to stick around, but she did.

"I'm done nailing. Do you have any more for me to do?" Todd asked, his hard hat slipping over his forehead.

Luke marked out where the next nails were to go on the board he had just tacked down. "This should keep you busy." Luke plucked the hard hat off the boy's head and adjusted the straps. "Here, that should stay on better."

Todd knocked himself on the head, then grinned at Luke. "I'm helping you good, aren't I?"

"You're doing a great job." Luke pulled a handkerchief out of his pocket, wiped a bead of sweat from his forehead and returned Todd's smile. "Now remember that you put the nails pointy side down, okay?"

Todd laughed and nodded as he bent down and started flailing away with his hammer.

"When you're done, Todd, you and Autumn have to get ready for bed," Janie said.

"But it's Sunday tomorrow."

"That's why you and Autumn need to be in bed on time."

Todd wrinkled his nose but kept nailing as Janie walked carefully past them, down the temporary step Luke had put together and pried a protesting Autumn from the swing set.

To Luke's surprise, when she came back, Todd got up and walked over to Luke, giving him his hammer. Then he followed his mother into the porch. He couldn't get over how obedient her kids were.

They left, and the yard felt deflated. As if the life had slipped out of it with the kids.

He smiled at the whimsy and finished nailing Todd's board down. This was all very domestic, and if he let himself, he could easily slide into the fantasy.

Husband working on the house. Wife and kids inside. He heard the sounds of water running, coming through an open window above him, then the murmuring sounds of Janie talking to the kids, tucking them in. Then her voice seemed to change cadence, soften.

Feeling like an intruder, Luke strained to listen even so.

Janie was praying with the kids.

Just like she had when he made chili the night she sprained her ankle.

He went back to nailing, his hands moving automatically as his thoughts skipped back to memories of Al teaching him to pray, bringing him along to church. He thought of the Bible he had packed along with all the other books in his trailer.

He had pulled it out the night he and Janie had talked. He thought of what she said about God being a loving and faithful Father.

Though he kept the Bible beside his bed, he hadn't opened it yet. He wanted to read the Bible for the right reasons. Not because a woman he was interested in read the Bible.

At one time, he had felt as if God had touched his life. Had been a part of his life.

But his own preoccupation with making a living, the busyness of his work had distracted him. And when Al died, Luke felt as if God had played a cruel joke on him. Giving him a father, then taking him away.

"Are you sure you don't need anything?" Janie's voice broke into his thoughts. She was back.

"Sorry," she said, "Didn't mean to startle you."

"No problem." Luke glanced over the deck, then up at the windows above. "I should quit anyway. I don't want to keep the kids awake."

Janie shook her head. "Do you hear that horrible sound that just started up in Suzie's room?"

"Some tortured form of rock and roll, I'm guessing," he said with a smile as the noise blasted through the quiet. He was surprised Janie let her daughter get away with listening to that.

"Todd and Autumn sleep through that, so I'm sure your nailing won't bother them."

"So in spite of all your protests to the contrary, you do want me to keep going?" Luke said with a teasing smile.

"No. No. I mean, you've done so much already. And I'm sure I could find someone to finish up—"

"I was kidding," Luke said, letting her off the hook. "I'll

come by and finish it Monday morning while you're at work. Because, as you pointed out, tomorrow is Sunday and it wouldn't do to work on the Sabbath." He dropped his hammer in his pouch and began gathering up the nails Autumn had scattered over the deck.

"But working on your house won't count?"

Luke shot her a frown, then realized it was her turn to tease him. "I probably shouldn't."

"But what would you do instead?"

Luke dropped the nails and the hammer Todd had been using in the toolbox he had brought along. "I don't know. Maybe read one of the dozens of books I packed along."

"What do you like to read?"

"Legal thrillers, psychology books, history, biographies, murder mysteries. How about you?"

"I don't read as much as I used to." She sounded wistful, and he assumed between the coffee shop and raising three kids she didn't have a lot of spare time.

Luke closed the lid on the toolbox. "I noticed Todd likes reading as well."

Janie sighed. "I sometimes wish he would get his nose out of his books and play."

"What do you mean? I've seen him play."

Janie gave him a rueful smile. "Because he likes being around you. You've made some kind of connection—" she stopped there, as if she didn't want to admit what she was about to say.

He didn't press the matter, but felt a tiny glow of satisfaction at what she said. "I like Todd. He's a fun kid. And Autumn seemed okay with Cooper."

"She's definitely getting better." Janie granted him another smile.

"I'm glad about that." He piled up the leftover lumber against the deck, then as he glanced over her way was surprised to see her watching him.

"You've been good for my kids," she said quietly.

Luke held her gaze, and once again, he felt it. The connection between them that tipped his hope into yearning. Without even realizing how, he now stood in front of her, their gazes tangling as the world wheeled and slowed.

She looked away from him. But she didn't move when he touched her shoulder. He squeezed lightly, solidifying the connection.

Her lack of movement gave him encouragement, and he decided to intrude just a little more into her life. "When I came by the other night, I heard you talking to Cooper."

Janie gave a short laugh, shaking her head. "Just babbling."

"I overheard what you said." He was quiet a moment, waiting for her protest, but when none came, he pressed on. "I thought your business was doing very well."

"It is." She bit her lip, then moved away. But she only went to sit down in one of the plastic chairs pushed against house. Luke sat in the one beside her.

"But…"

Janie heaved a sigh, staring out over the yard. "It's not really your concern. It's my problem, and I shouldn't burden you."

He sensed she was trying to convince herself more than inform him. "Does this have anything to do with the visit you made to the banker the other week?" he asked, gently prompting her.

She nodded, wrapping arms around her midsection, as if trying to hold everything in. But then she took a quick breath. "I've been wallowing in my operating loan too long and I've renegotiated too many times. I'm losing equity in the business, and the building is for sale. I'd hoped to make an audacious business decision and buy it, but the loan was turned down because I can't get out of my operating loan. So you see, it's a vicious circle."

"And the bank is going to call in the loan? So how did you get this far behind?"

This elicited another sigh. "Owen. My ex-husband."

"I thought you were widowed."

"We were married for nine years, divorced for two. He died eighteen months ago."

This time Luke didn't say anything, giving her the space he sensed she needed to sort through her thoughts and decide which ones she would share.

"He worked the rigs, made good money. But on his way home he started spending time at the casinos. He worked his way through a lot of the money he made and then started piling up debts on credit cards. I started the coffee shop out of necessity. I needed a way to make money separate from him, and I wanted the independence of my own business." Janie sighed, releasing her grip on her waist as she pleated her fingers together. "The trouble was, I needed the equity from the house for collateral on the loan. And the more Owen spent, the less collateral the house had. I was actually glad he left me, you know."

"I can imagine," Luke murmured, her story sounding all too familiar. "But your business is doing well."

"It is. But Owen didn't mind borrowing from my father. And paying him back was my first priority. My father didn't know what a sacrifice it was for me, and I never told him. And private loans don't show up in financial statements."

"But they should show up in cash flow."

"I thought so, too. And I thought that would count for

something when I decided to buy the building the coffee shop is located in."

"I noticed the For Sale sign the other day."

"I wanted to expand. I thought rather than try to convince the bank to extend the loan, I would be aggressive. Make a bold move." She gave a bitter laugh. "My banker suggested I talk to my father."

"Oh, of course. Run to Daddy," he said with a measure of anger. "Can't believe he suggested that."

Janie's eyes met his, and in her sad smile, he sensed approval. "Me, either."

"So what's next?"

Janie looked away, breaking the connection, her eyes wandering over the immaculate yard. "I've spent the last few weeks pouring all my extra energy into my expansion plan. Now? I don't know."

"What were you going to do with the rest of the building?" he asked, curious about her plans.

Her smile held a touch of wistful melancholy. "I've always wanted to have a bookstore. All those shelves of brand-new books, waiting for an owner. If I owned the building, I thought I could knock out part of the wall so people could go back and forth between the two. I'd add a craft section and maybe some supplies. Make it more than just a bookstore. Make it a community place. I know it would get patronized in this town, especially in combination with my coffee shop." She gave him a sheepish smile. "Sorry. It was nice to dream, but that's all it is now."

He held her gaze, envisioning the concept, imagining her walking along shelves of books, trailing her fingers along them. For a moment he was jealous of her plans. They showed stability. Recognizing her community and contributing to it. He wished he could do something like that.

"I wish, for your sake and for the sake of Riverbend, it could happen. I know I'd be a good customer." He shared her smile, then touched her arm again, as if to console her in the loss of her dreams. "I'm a sucker for books."

Janie turned to him, her eyes lighting up. "Me, too. I have a 'to be read' list as long as my arm."

"That's not that long." Luke said with a grin, picking up her hand to extend her arm. He stretched his out beside hers. "Now that would be a long 'to be read' list."

Their eyes held, and to his surprise, she touched his arm with her fingers, solidifying the connection. "Not everyone understands that."

"Anyone who reads does. I'm sure Todd does."

Janie's expression grew clouded, and she looked down at his hand. "Todd retreats to his books. They're like an escape for him."

"I'm sure things have been confusing for him. First his father leaves, then he dies. I know I wanted to escape when my father died. And I was thirty-some years old."

Janie didn't say anything, her eyes still downcast. In the background, Luke heard the noises of the neighborhood settling in. Across the alley a mother called a child in. The last warning, she said. A dog barked. Cooper joined in.

Families in a neighborhood and each home had their own stories.

"I tried to shield him," Janie said. "Tried to shield all the kids. But it seems…" her words faded away.

"You've done what you can, I'm sure. I've said it before, you're a good mother to your kids."

She looked up, and as their eyes met, he felt as if he had been knocked back by the longing in her gaze. Longing that matched his own.

"Janie," he whispered, leaning closer.

"I'm going to church tomorrow," she said quietly.

Luke stumbled mentally as he tried to catch up to where she was going. He sat back, frustrated by the shift in the atmosphere, yet sensing this needed to be dealt with if he wanted any chance with her.

"You still think I should go?" he asked, keeping his tone light and carefree.

"For your own sake."

"I've read that God reveals Himself through the Word and through creation. I could just sit out on my lawn or go to the beach and let Him reveal Himself to me. That would be just as good."

Janie caught his tone and returned his smile. "You could. But no one at the beach, or on your lawn for that matter, is going to confront you with your sin or your need for a Savior. Which is what happens at church."

"You're not a theologian."

"I'm a sinner in need of grace," Janie said, her tone suddenly serious.

"You don't seem like a sinner to me," he said quietly.

Janie gave him a rueful smile. "Then you don't know me very well."

"I know you well enough that I admire who you are and what you've done with your kids."

She kept her eyes on his, and her smile softened. "You're a good man, Luke."

Her words encouraged him to take another chance. He slipped his finger under her chin. She didn't pull away. Didn't protest. Instead she sat as still as a statue as if waiting.

He bent over and brushed his lips over hers.

She tasted sweet. Like the iced tea she liked to drink. His

hand drifted to her shoulder, held on, wanting to build on the slight connection.

Her hand came up and touched his face, and then he couldn't stop himself. He pulled her close, wrapped his arms around her, protecting her, laying his claim on her.

He kissed her again while he felt his heart beating in his neck, in his chest, in the hands that held her close.

When she drew away, his only surprise was that she hadn't done it sooner.

"I'm sorry," she whispered. "I shouldn't have let you do that."

He knew where she was coming from. He understood. But he was also getting tired of it.

"I'm not a fly-by-night kind of guy, Janie. I know you're scared. I am too. But the only way we're going to find out if this will work is if you let me into your life. Just a little at a time."

He waited, as expectation hovered between them.

"And your house?"

At first he didn't know what she meant and then it came to him. The very presence of his trailer on the yard was a reminder to her that he was here only temporarily.

"It's not my house, Janie. I bought it with a partner."

"So you're going to be selling it."

Luke stood up, moving away from her, his frustration with her and with their situation spilling out. "What do you want, Janie? What am I supposed to do? I kiss you and you push me away. I try to be a part of your life and you won't let me. I know where you're at. I get that you've got to protect your kids, but in order for me to make any kind of commitment, in order to know whether what we shared is going to go anywhere, I need something from you, too."

Janie looked away and stayed silent.

Luke looked down at her, then left.

Chapter Fourteen

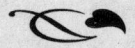

And you are going to church because?

Luke silenced the critical voice in his head as he listened to the worship band finish their last song.

He knew he had to separate his growing feelings for Janie from his deepening relationship with the Lord.

He knew that he was trying to find his way through this new place he had come to, and he knew that church was a vital part of that.

That much, he had learned from Al. His foster father had always told him that though one could worship anywhere, it was only in church that you were confronted with the daily need for forgiveness. And it was only in church that you received the nourishment you needed from fellow believers.

And one of those fellow believers—he wasn't going to lie—was Janie.

As he sat down, Luke glanced around the congregation again. He hadn't seen Janie or her kids yet. One woman had caught his eye. In profile she looked a lot like Janie, but she was a blonde, had a baby and a husband.

He had seen Janie's mother standing beside a patrician-looking gentleman Luke assumed was Janie's father.

But no Janie.

The minister stood up again and invited the congregation to open their Bibles to Luke 6. He started reading, and as Luke followed along, he thought of the Bible lying beside his bed. After he and Janie had talked on the porch, he had gone back to his trailer and opened it up, starting at the New Testament.

"….Do not judge, and you will not be judged," the minister was saying. "Do not condemn, and you will not be condemned. Forgive, and you will be forgiven."

The words jumped out at Luke.

Forgive. Forgive his mother.

While the pastor carried on, Luke reread the words of the passage.

Luke knew he was in need of forgiveness. He hadn't been following God's will for his life the past few years. But he hadn't caused anyone any harm. As much as possible he'd tried to live so that his father would be proud of him. So that he could stand before God unashamed.

"Forgive and you will be forgiven."

The words surrounded him, pulled at the barriers he had put up against his mother.

She didn't deserve his forgiveness.

But do you deserve God's?

He tried to pull his righteous anger around him, like a cloak of protection against what he was reading.

"Our sins are like a chasm between us and God," the pastor was saying. "Forgiveness is the bridge. But until we forgive others, we cannot truly believe the forgiveness of God for our own sins. We can't embrace the idea that we have been forgiven and live lives of forgiveness. Too often we hold the offenses of people close because it's easier than recognizing our own faults before God. To know that none of us can stand blameless before Him is a hard thing to accept. God's forgiveness is not conditional upon our forgiving others but our pride, which keeps us from forgiving others, can also keep us from accepting God's forgiveness. But until we both receive and give forgiveness, we are bound by the hurts others have inflicted on us. When we forgive, we are free."

Luke grew still as the pastor's words piled on top of the Bible passage he had just read.

He knew in his head what had to happen, but how could he forget all the hurts his mother had truly inflicted on him? How could he forgive when she had never, once, asked him for forgiveness? Never had shown, in any way, that she was sorry?

Luke closed the Bible and sat back, troubled by what he read. By what he heard. He had to think this over. He'd struggled with his feelings for his mother so long; it would take more than a sermon to make him change his mind.

He crossed his arms over his chest, waiting for the pastor to be done, waiting for the moment when he could see Janie again. Wondering if he had read too much in her response.

"Cappuccinos all around *and* muffins?" Janie handed Luke his order with a smile. "What are you and the crew celebrating?"

"The end of the job," Luke said, handing her two twenties.

She almost dropped the money. "That soon? I thought you were running behind." If the house was finished that meant…

"I'm still behind. But I finished your deck this morning, then I officially told the crew today was their last day."

"So what…how?" Janie tried to parse her confusion as she kept her hands busy, wiping off the steamer, rinsing the metal cup the milk was in.

"How am I going to finish it in time?" Luke took the box of muffins and the tray with the coffee cups and winked at her. "I cancelled the open house."

Janie frowned, still not sure what was going on.

"I talked to my partner. I'm thinking we won't go through with the sale of the house."

Janie held his gaze and in his eyes read a deeper meaning to what he was saying. And hope stirred in her heart.

"What would you do?"

"I'm thinking I might buy out his half."

"And then?"

Luke shrugged. "Seek gainful employment. I noticed the co-op is hiring. Or I could start another business."

"So we might be neighbors."

"Good neighbors, I hope."

Janie slowly wiped down the machine, trying to choose her next words. "I saw you in church on Sunday."

"I didn't see you."

"The kids and I had to help one of the Sunday School teachers right after the service. I went out the front."

"And I was in the back."

"I'm glad you went."

"Yeah. Me, too." His smile held a promise, and he looked as if he was about to say more when the door to the shop jangled and a group of men wearing suits entered.

Luke stepped aside as he tossed off a wave. "Gotta go now."

While Janie took the men's orders, most of her attention was on Luke, glancing over as he left the shop then catching a glimpse of him getting into his truck. Cooper sat on the seat beside him, inspecting the box Luke put between them.

Luke started the truck, then caught her watching him. His mouth lifted in a lazy smile full of promise.

"I said I wanted a latte," one of the men complained.

"Sorry. I wasn't paying attention." Normally she'd be flustered by the mistake, but now it didn't matter.

The sheaf of papers on the table behind her outlining her latest save-the-coffee-shop scheme didn't matter either. Nor did they seem as ominous and depressing as they had the previous few days.

She had gone over figures until her eyes were crossed. There was no way out, Though she'd fought her next decision for so long, she knew letting go of the coffee shop was the right thing to do.

She felt a momentary flutter of fear. Then she took a breath.

Help me, Lord, to let go. To stop fighting. To trust that You will take care of me and my children. To trust that whatever happens, You are in control. Not me.

The morning dragged on heavy feet as the clock ticked toward noon. Janie closed up the shop, walked over to the bank and marched inside.

Ten minutes later she stood in the afternoon sun, feeling the tension, which had held her shoulders taut for the past few weeks, ease away. The panic made another brief appearance, but she breathed it away.

It was done.

Janie returned to the shop with a sense of lightness and expectation. She thought of Luke, and the irony of his starting over in Riverbend just as she was making moves to close her business.

A cluster of people stood by the door, peering into the shop, looking puzzled. As Janie approached them, she wondered where they were going to get their coffee now.

Not your worry, she reminded herself as she unlocked the shop and began serving.

Though the rest of the afternoon seemed to fly, by the time

Janie was ready to close the shop, her ankle was sore once again, and a niggling of worry had returned.

She locked the door and was about to turn the sign over when her father appeared at the door. He wore an open necked golf shirt and khakis. He must have been out at the golf course.

Puzzled as to why he would come here, she unlocked it and let him in.

"Hey, Dad. A little late for coffee, isn't it?"

"It is. I was hoping I could talk to you."

"You want to come to the house?"

Her father shook his head, his blue eyes concentrating on hers. "I prefer to talk to you without the kids around."

Janie locked the door, turned the sign around and sat at the nearest table. Her father sat down across from her and folded his hands on the table, much as he used to whenever he had something important to say.

Janie's heart flipped over slowly at the frown wrinkling her father's brow.

"What's wrong, Dad?"

"You're not allowed to get angry. You're not allowed to fuss, but I just played a round of golf with Victor."

Janie didn't fuss, but she did get angry, guessing where this was going. "And what did my account manager have to say to you?"

"He told me what you did today. Told me what dire straits you were in."

"Not so dire, Daddy." Not as far as the coffee shop was concerned.

"He also told me that at one time you were hoping to buy the building. Expand the business."

What *didn't* Victor tell her father?

"Also right." Janie resisted the urge to fiddle with the sugar container beside her hand. She felt a curious combination of guilt and relief. Relief that her father now knew and guilt that she hadn't told him earlier.

"I stopped by the real estate agent. I wanted to talk to her about purchasing the entire building."

"Daddy. You didn't." She had made up her mind. She had made her decision. It was over. "I don't need you riding in at the last minute to rescue me."

"Doesn't matter. I can't. Someone else made an offer on the building this morning."

This was news and, to be honest, a bit of a relief. That particular avenue was firmly closed, as well. "Well, that's that."

"Not really. What are you going to do?" Dan Westerveld's expression shifted, and Janie read pain and worry in his face.

"I'm going to be okay. I have a little bit of equity left. I can find a job pretty quickly."

"Working at the Inn? Waitressing?"

"If I have to. I could also take night classes. Finish my degree. Become a teacher." Janie gave her dad a reassuring smile. "I'm not a dummy. I could learn. I'm still young. I've got one year of college behind me."

"And there's no room in your life for anyone else?"

Janie thought of Luke and smiled. "I had to make a decision, and I'm at peace with it. I've prayed about it, and about the coffee shop. I know I have to stop fighting. Stop trying so hard to make this work."

If she thought too much about the future, if she started speculating too much, the dread could return, but for now, she trusted that God was guiding her decision.

Dan reached across the table and covered her hands with his. "I would gladly have given you what you needed if you'd only asked."

"I know, Daddy. But I had my own obligations and duties, and you taught me and Dodie to be responsible with them. And I like to think I have."

"When you said you wanted to pay me back, I had no idea that this was only a small portion of the debt Owen had run up."

"I guess I didn't tell you because I was ashamed. I'm a proud person. I wanted to make this work on my own." Janie drew in a deep breath. "But that's over. I've made up my mind and to tell you the truth, Daddy, I feel free. I know I've got a tough road ahead of me, but I feel as if I can do this. I can get a job. I can support my family."

Luke's unspoken promise lingered in her mind, and she clung to the hope in it. She wasn't alone. Not anymore.

Dan smiled at his daughter. "You were always such an independent miss. I thought that might have changed. But I guess not." He got up, walked around the table and dropped a kiss on her head. "I'll be praying for you and the kids. And I know you might not like hearing this, but I'm still going to pray that someday someone might come into your life."

Janie's mind slipped to Luke.

And she wondered.

Chapter Fifteen

The kids were in bed. The sun was slipping below the horizon.

And the lights were on in Luke's house. He must be working on it, Janie thought, a trickle of anticipation dancing down her spine as she stood on the newly finished deck.

He wasn't going to sell the house. He was staying.

She touched her lips, resurrecting once again the kiss he had given her on this very spot as the scent of newly cut wood wafted around her.

She glanced over at the house, and as she did, felt a flutter of anticipation at the thought of seeing him. A smile tilted her mouth.

The phone rang, and with an irritated sigh at the interruption she turned away, back to the house.

It was her mother.

"Honey, your father told me what you did." Tilly's voice was shrill. Angry. "You can't stop running your coffee shop. It's your business."

Janie sat back as she tried to let her mother's emotions slide over her. She couldn't let the frustration or sorrow in her mother's voice deter her from the decision she had made.

"Surely you can let us help you," she said. "We can't let you lose this business. I know this will be a huge disappointment."

A disappointment for me or for you?

"…and goodness knows, we've all had enough disappointments."

Her mother's words piled on Janie's shoulders, each one adding to the burden of guilt Janie struggled to shrug off each day.

"I'm sorry you feel that way, Mom, but I don't want Dad's help. I don't want to keep the coffee shop going that way."

"But, Janie, how will this look?"

And there lay the crux of the matter. Bad enough that Janie had to get married. Bad enough that Owen turned out to be such a loser. Bad enough that he divorced her.

Now this had to be added to the mix? Successful businessman Dan Westerveld's own daughter couldn't keep her own business?

"It will look like I tried to do what I could, but it didn't work. That's what it will look like."

Her mother's theatrical sigh made Janie want to scream in frustration. Give me some credit, Mom, she wanted to cry. Recognize what I *have* done. What I *have* accomplished.

"Are you sure your father couldn't—"

"Positive, Mom." Janie clenched the phone as she stepped out the door. She looked at Luke's house, suddenly yearning to talk to him. To lay her head on his shoulder and let him hold her up.

"I have to go, Mom," she said, her decision made for her by her own needs. "See you later." And before her mother could add more guilt to the mix, Janie hung up.

Then she dropped the phone on a chair on the deck, stepped down from the deck and walked across the soft grass, her heart lifting at the thought of seeing Luke.

She stepped through a hole in the hedge, then paused when she saw a woman standing by a car, parked across the street.

In the gathering dusk, Janie couldn't see her face but, now and again, caught the glow of a cigarette.

As Janie glanced her way, the woman pushed herself away from the car and flicked the cigarette. She shoved her hands into the pockets of her short leather coat, her eyes on Janie.

Janie glanced over at the house, but all she heard was the muffled pounding of a hammer. Luke was working.

As she walked over the cool, dampening grass the woman came toward her. Janie felt a frisson of fear, but dampened it down. The woman didn't look as if she weighed more than 110 pounds.

"Hi, there," the woman said as she came near. "You don't know me, but I know who you are."

This was creepy.

"And you are…" Janie asked, suddenly tense.

The woman gave her a crooked smile. "Lillian Harris. Luke's mom."

Janie felt the words hit her like a blow. "I see."

"He told you about me, didn't he?" Her voice was hoarse, and as she spoke, she coughed.

Janie nodded.

"Luke's inside the house?"

"Yes. Are you going in?"

Lillian tilted her head as if to study Janie from another angle. "Are you?"

"Yes. I am."

"You his girlfriend or something?"

"I live next door."

Lillian pulled her lower lip between her teeth, scraping off the red lipstick. "He won't talk to me, but maybe he'll listen to you." She reached inside her coat and handed Janie a thick letter-sized envelope. "Can you give this to him? He doesn't have to call me or anything. But I want him to have this."

"I think it would be better if you gave it to him yourself," Janie said, unsure she should take it.

Lillian gave a short laugh, then started coughing again. "Trust me, he won't let me in the house." She waved the envelope at Janie. "Please. Give it to him? I just need to clear this up."

Janie responded to the pleading in her voice. "Okay. I'll give it to him."

Lillian started walking backward. "Thanks. Thanks a bunch." She gave Janie a heavyhearted smile. "He's a good guy. I just…" The words trailed off into the night as Lillian turned around, waited for a car to pass, then walked across the street to her car.

Janie waited, watching as she got into the car, then drove away, her taillights winking as she slowed for the corner at the end of the street.

As quickly as she came, Luke's mother was gone.

Janie tapped the envelope against her other hand, wondering what it held. A letter? An apology?

She looked down the now-empty street, still trying to process the odd meeting. Luke's mother.

Janie turned and walked to the house.

The door wasn't locked, and as she opened it, she heard the scrambling of claws on the floor. She quickly stepped inside and was almost bowled over by the body of an over-enthusiastic dog.

"Cooper. Down," she commanded as she stepped into the house. The smell of paint combined with the smell of strong glue stung her nostrils.

She glanced into the living room. The floor was still bare

wood, but the walls now glowed a pale sage-green. She mentally finished the room, hung some pictures and installed furniture. It would be a beautiful, welcoming room when it was done.

"Hello? Someone there?" Luke's voice made her heart dance in her chest.

"Just me," she called back, following his voice into the kitchen, Cooper trotting behind her.

Luke looked up from the board he was cutting, unbuckled his carpenter's pouch and as it dropped with a thunk, he gave her a slow, gentle smile. "So, what do you think of the place?"

Janie looked around, appreciating the pale, buttery yellow of the kitchen walls. Some of the cabinets had been installed already, their golden brown wood gleaming in the track lighting from the ceiling. "So far, it's beautiful."

"I think so, too." Luke brushed the sawdust off one of the cupboards. "I'm still trying to decide if I should go with laminate flooring or tile in here?"

"Tile can be hard on the knees," Janie said.

"Laminate it is."

Janie looked around, trying to imagine it finished. "You've done a lot with this place already. I'm impressed."

"That's good. I was going for amazed, but I'm happy with impressed." He gave her a lopsided smile. "Did you just pick up your mail?"

Janie glanced down at the envelope she was holding. "No. Actually, I just got this from your mom."

His smile was replaced by a frown. "When did you see her?"

"Just now. She was standing in front of the house. Like she was trying to work up enough courage to come in."

Luke's expression grew tight as Janie handed him the envelope. He tossed it on the countertop without a second glance.

"You're not going to look at it?"

Luke shook his head.

"She seemed sad, Luke. I think she wants to see you again."

He simply shrugged.

"Don't you want to talk about her?"

"No. I don't. She doesn't matter."

"How can you say that?" Janie felt uneasy at the bitterness in his voice.

"They're simple words for a simple truth. She messed up. She had a chance and she ruined it."

"How?"

Luke sighed and shook his head. "You're such a good mother. Such a caring person. I don't think you'd understand her."

Janie could have left everything alone, could have taken his word for what he said. But her relationship with Luke was shifting. She didn't want any surprises. "Try me," she said, touching his arm as if to encourage him. "Tell me about your relationship with your mother."

"The truth is, she didn't want me, Janie. I was an inconvenience to her. You wouldn't understand that. Not you."

The unease clenched as his words pried at the box holding her own particular guilt and shame.

"How do you know?" She eased the words past lips that had grown stiff.

"Because of who you are. What your kids are like. You have a strong relationship with them. Something I've always wanted from my own mother but never got." He touched her cheek. "In spite of your difficult marriage, you desperately wanted and cared for each one of your kids. But my mother? To her I was something to be discarded."

Each word dug deep into old scars, old secrets.

"Was she alone when she found out she was expecting you?" Janie asked.

"Why are we even talking about her?"

"If she was alone, maybe she was afraid."

"Why are you defending her?" Luke's eyebrows came together in an angry *V*. "She doesn't deserve to be defended."

"She could have gotten rid of you before you were born, but she didn't do that, did she?"

"Things might have been better if she had. As it was, I experienced her precise feelings toward me every day. And every day I felt less and less worthy. And even when I was put in a foster home, she kept ruining things. Again and again."

The words fell between them, like heavy stones. Stones that, it seemed to Janie, slowly accumulated, added to by his anger and her guilt. She pulled her hand away from his, lowered her head.

"She didn't want me, Janie," he continued, the anger still tingeing his voice. "I can't seem to get past that. I can't let go. What kind of mother can even feel that way?"

"Can you forgive her?" Janie kept her focus on the dust on the floor.

"I don't know."

Janie swallowed the bile in her throat, her own past darkening the discussion. Her heart hurt, and she could feel the pain of her past easing, once again, into her life.

He couldn't imagine being with someone like his mother. *She* was like his mother.

"I have to go," she said quietly, trying to slip past him. She couldn't be here anymore. Couldn't listen to his angry words condemning a woman she could have turned into.

"Why?"

"If you feel that way about your own mother …"

Luke shook his head. "No. Don't you even go there. What I feel for my mother has nothing to do with us."

"That's where you're wrong, Luke. It has everything to do with us." Janie couldn't look at him. Couldn't face him.

"What are you saying? Why won't you look at me?"

"I have to go," she added, though the words cut her even more deeply than his. "I can't be here."

"Because of my mother? Because of how I feel about her? Because I don't want to let myself get hurt by her yet again?"

The pain in his voice was almost her undoing. But if he found out, if he knew, she couldn't face his disappointment with her.

"Now you're hiding behind my relationship with my mother," he continued. "Just like you were hiding behind your relationship with your kids. You're looking for excuses. Why don't you admit it?"

Janie heard his words on one level and felt them on another. She felt the secret she had harbored all these years, pushing to be given shape, form. She had kept it to herself so long, she wondered what it would feel like to let it out.

Janie shook her head. "It isn't an excuse, Luke."

"Then what is it?" He threw his hands out to the side in frustration.

Janie threw her arm up to protect her face, but as quickly as she reacted, she corrected herself.

Just in time to see the absolute devastation her reflexive action created in Luke's expression. He took a step away from her, as if to give her the distance he seemed to think she needed.

"Janie. No. I would never, ever…"

She felt suddenly foolish. "I know that. I'm sorry."

"You've got to believe me, Janie." The anger in his voice had dissipated and was replaced with anguish.

She reached out to touch him, to reassure him.

And he caught her in his arms, holding her close. "I shouldn't have been so angry with you, Janie. My mother is just a side road. I don't want to talk about her. She's out of my life. She's not important."

And that's where he was wrong.

For a moment, Janie allowed herself the luxury of leaning on him, of feeling his arms surrounding her, of clinging to his strength, of allowing a few might-have-beens into the emptiness that had been her life before Luke and his goofy dog burst in. Then she reluctantly drew away.

"Your mother is important, Luke. At least how you feel about her is important." Janie focused on the third button of his flannel shirt as she spoke, on the specks of sawdust sprinkling his shirt. "You need to understand where she is coming from. I think you need to take some time to talk to her."

Now it was Luke's turn to be silent. She felt his arms drop away from her.

"Why do you say that?" He almost growled the words out, and for a moment Janie wished she hadn't said anything, but she had felt an urge to explain, to help him understand

"She's a mother. I know what that feels like." She kept her eyes straight ahead as she prayed for strength to tell him. "And being a mother never changes. I'm sure she loves you and wishes she had done things differently."

"You don't know anything about my situation, Janie. Don't presume to tell me what I have to do."

"I heard the same sermon you did, Luke. If you believe, as you told me you did the other night, then as a Christian you have to forgive her, don't you?" Janie put out this appeal on a whisper.

His silence seemed to push at her, to create a distance between them. She held his eyes, trying to find even the smallest spark of forgiveness in them.

"Mothers don't abandon their kids, Janie. You know that better than anyone."

He reached for her again, but she stepped away.

"We're not perfect, Luke. We're not this wonderful, magical family. We're messy, and we have secrets and problems." She threw her arguments out trying to plug up the cracks in her defenses. If he knew…

"What problems?" He looked genuinely baffled. "You go to church, you have a sincere faith. Thanks to you, your kids are some of the best-behaved kids I've ever seen."

"No, Luke, it's not thanks to me. It's only God's grace. I love my kids, but I don't deserve them."

Luke frowned, as if what her words were finally registering. "What do you mean?"

They stood across from each other as an expectant silence filled the room.

She finally broke it. "You may think you want what I have, but what you are seeking is only an illusion, Luke. It's just a dream that you've foisted on my family. And when you find out the truth, the dream will die. We're not the family for you, Luke. We're not."

Then she turned away from him and walked out of his house.

Chapter Sixteen

She had done the right thing, Janie reminded herself as she sat cross-legged on her bed, the Bible open on her lap. She had been right to stop what was growing between her and Luke.

She couldn't have borne to see his reaction when he found out the truth.

He might have been able to deal with it.

On the heels of that optimistic thought came the sound of Luke's voice when he spoke about the woman who had given birth to him. And how he spoke about her. As if they were two completely different entities.

Oh, Luke, she thought, you were embracing a dream, not me. And if he were to find out the mess that really was her life, she would be a disappointment to him, too.

And that, she simply couldn't bear.

She turned to Isaiah 49:15.

"Can a mother forget the baby at her breast and have no compassion on the child she has borne?"

Janie had heard the passage in church when she was expecting Suzie, and it had haunted her. Each time she opened the Bible, she caught herself turning to it, as if picking at a sore.

The second part of the verse and verse sixteen had given her some small comfort, "…Though she may forget, I will not forget you. See, I have engraved you on the palms of my hands; your walls are ever before me."

Against her will, her mind skipped back to the first moment she found out she was expecting Suzie. How she had wanted to sweep her own child out of her life. When she knew she couldn't do that, her next thought was adoption.

She hadn't wanted her own child either. And she knew she couldn't tell Luke that. She preferred that he nurture this idea of a perfect woman with the perfect family, rather than see his expression when he would find out she was no different than his mother.

Luke wiped the last bit of drywall dust off the wall and dropped the sander into the box on the floor. He had worked late into the night, as he had for the past week, and he was finally done.

Tomorrow the plumber was coming to install the sinks and hook up the water, and the day after that, the linoleum and carpet people would arrive and then the house would be finished.

Luke walked the length of the house, then turned through the arched doorway into the kitchen, his booted feet echoing in the emptiness of the house.

When he moved from the trailer into the house, he felt as if he had made a huge step toward settling. Toward creating a home.

He'd made up some silly dreams about this place, he thought, as he walked into the kitchen. Dreams that had included a few more renovations to the upstairs bedroom and the master bedroom downstairs. A housewarming party that included the family next door. The family he had pinned his hopes on. The woman he had grown to love.

I love you.

The words, spoken in this very room, seemed to mock him now.

What was he thinking? Janie had her standards and her life, and there wasn't room in it for a man who had flotsam and jetsam from his past floating around.

He heard the tick of claws behind him and turned to see Cooper drop onto the floor. "I haven't been a whole lot of company lately, have I?" Luke said, crouching down to stroke his dog's head.

Cooper's only reply was a lift of one eye, which gave him a quizzical look.

He stepped out onto the back deck, and against his better judgment, he glanced over at Janie's house.

A light shone out of her bedroom window. It was eleven o'clock at night and she was still up.

He wanted to look away, to act as if he didn't care that she was going to be tired when she got up tomorrow morning in time to get the kids ready for school. He didn't need to be involved in any part of her life; she didn't want him there.

But what she wanted and what actually happened seemed to be two different things. He wanted to brush her out of his life, but he couldn't.

Each time he walked past the window looking out over their yard, he checked to see if the kids were playing outside. And each time his cell phone rang, he hoped that it might be her. Each time he went to town, he slowed down by her coffee shop. Yesterday he noticed the closed sign. He heard, via other townspeople, that she was letting it go, and he yearned to talk to her about that.

"Well, I guess it's bedtime for us, mister," he said to Cooper, rubbing the dog's head. "Tomorrow is a another day."

He walked through the kitchen, then down the hall to the master bedroom. Good thing he hadn't bought out his partner as soon as he'd hoped. Now they could sell the place and he could move on.

Cooper dropped onto his dog bed and laid his head on his paws, watching as Luke picked up a pile of papers he had just gotten from the bank, outlining his most recent scheme.

He glanced them over, then dropped them back on the chair he was using as an end table.

As he did, he caught sight of the envelope his mother had given him. He had thrown it aside, and in the busyness of pushing his neighbor aside through overwork, he had forgotten about it.

He sat on the edge of his bed, thinking of what Janie had said, recalling the sermon he had heard a few Sundays ago.

Forgiveness. Janie thought his lack of forgiveness toward his mother had something to do with her. He couldn't make the connection, but at the same time, ever since the sermon he heard on Sunday, ever since his confrontation with Janie, he kept thinking about forgiveness.

He pulled his Bible off the end table and turned to the concordance. There were a lot of verses written after the word *forgive*. So he turned to one. Colossians 3:13. "Bear with each other and forgive whatever grievances you may have against one another. Forgive as the Lord forgave you."

The words lay heavy on his conscience. He knew he had been forgiven much. His foster father had reminded him of that daily. The sermon he heard on Sunday underlined it.

But this wasn't a mere grievance he'd had to deal with. His legacy from his mother was flat out rejection again and again.

Then why does she keep coming back? Keep calling?

That was easy. Every time she called, every time she came, she wanted money. But even as he answered his own question, doubts remained. Doubts built upon the very slim hopes he had nurtured as a child. That someday she would come back into his life.

Would want him.

Forgive as the Lord forgave you.

Luke dropped back on the bed and stared at the ceiling.

I don't know if I have the strength for that, Lord. I don't know if I can.

My grace is sufficient for you.

As the words seeped into his mind, he thought of his accusation to Janie. Was he any less independent? Was he any less proud?

He thought he didn't need to forgive his mother. Thought he could live his life without her. But, as Janie had told him, mother and children are inextricably bound.

Luke dropped his head in his hands, mourning the loss of the day, struggling with what he had to do.

I want to do this for you, Lord. Not for Janie.

My grace is sufficient for you.

He opened the envelope and, along with a letter, a wad of one hundred dollar bills fell out.

Frowning, he unfolded the letter and began reading.

"I wanted to do this a long time ago," his mother wrote. "I never spent all the money you gave me. I just used it as an excuse. I was hoping I'd have a chance to tell you that I'm sorry whenever you transferred the money, but you never talked to me. I don't blame you. I know I've said it before, but I want to try again. I'm not strong, but I don't want to mess up. I have a job now, and I've been sober for two years, one month and five days. I don't want to mess up. Every day I pray God will help me. He has so far. If you don't want to see me, I get it."

Luke read and reread the letter, his old hurts, disappointments and pain weaving through the words. He put the letter down, read Colossians again, then began to pray. *Help me, Lord. Just like her, I can't do this on my own. I need Your help. And, Lord, please be with Janie. Comfort her. I'm sure she's having a hard time with her business now, too.* He stopped wondering if he had the right to add that last bit.

But in spite of what she told him, he still cared about her. Still thought of her. Still hurt each time he did.

Half an hour later he was out of town, headed to Kolvik where his mother was staying with an old friend.

When he pulled up in front of the house, he felt a mixture of fear and anticipation. As he walked to the door, he was surprised to feel his heart in his chest.

When he rang the bell and his mother answered the door, the first thing he did was look at her eyes. They were clear and held a faint spark of hope.

She didn't smell like beer or weed, and her smile was tentative. She looked as if she had no built-in expectations.

"Hi, Mom," he said.

"Hello, son," she replied, her voice thick with sorrow. "I've missed you."

"I've missed you, too," he said.

"I can't see why we can't have Melody babysit at the house," Suzie grumbled as Janie pulled up to her parent's house.

Janie didn't even bother trying to follow her child's convoluted reasoning. A few days ago she complained that Melody was bossy and before that, how much she liked going to Grandma and Grandpa's place.

Now, in the ever-shifting world of teenhood, she had suddenly decided the opposite.

"Don't forget your homework," she said to Suzie as she got out of the car. "Grandpa said he would help you with math."

"Did you tell Grandma that I have to stay to work on my science project after school today?"

"Yes. She said she would pick you up." Janie glanced at her watch. She didn't have to be at the shop at any particular time. All she had to do today was clean up, lock up and take the keys to the bank.

But she wanted it over and she wanted it done. The sooner the better. And the busyness of winding down the shop would keep her mind off Luke.

His name sent a needle of pain through her heart.

Stop. Stop.

"She doesn't have to pick me up," Suzie said. "Serena's dad said he would bring me home."

Janie paused at the door, looking back at Suzie. "What? This is new."

"I told you." Suzie's face took on that mutinous look that Janie had seen too often in the past couple of weeks.

It was as if she had picked up on Janie's mood and was channeling a younger, more intense version of it. She knew the kids missed Luke, too. The first few days they had asked about him, had wondered what was going on.

When she told them that he was busy, it seemed as if they caught the hidden meaning in her words. Todd retreated to his books, Autumn began carting her bear around and Suzie was even more ill-tempered than usual.

This was why she had tried to keep herself heart-whole, she thought, the pain in her heart over her own loss matching the pain she knew was in her children's. This was exactly what she had hoped to avoid. And she had failed miserably.

The needle twisted, and Janie swallowed the pain down as the door opened.

"You're late" were the first words out of her mother's mouth. "Well, come in children. Janie, you'd better get going. I'm sure you've got lots to do today."

Janie tried to ignore the veiled sarcasm as she kissed Autumn and Todd goodbye. Suzie had taken advantage of her momentary distraction to slip past her, neatly avoiding any chance for Janie to show her any type of affection.

So the cycle continues, Janie thought, remembering how Suzie was complaining, just the other day, that she consistently favored Todd and Autumn. That she loved them more.

Her words were like hot coals, burning through her head. Just what every struggling-with-guilt mother needs.

"I have an interview this afternoon, and I was hoping to clean the house, so I'll be by at nine o'clock to pick them up," Janie said just before her mother closed the door.

It would have been nice to get some words of encouragement, especially today of all days. Instead she got the full brunt of her mother's secondhand shame.

Janie turned and walked down the walk to her car. Unbidden came a picture of Luke behind the wheel.

So close, she thought, holding her hand to her chest, as if to contain the hurt in her heart. For a brief and beautiful moment, she had thought her life was moving in a good direction to a place she wanted to be.

With a man she wanted to be with.

She drove away from her parents' home to her shop downtown, parked her car and, for the last time, walked through the back door and into the shop.

As she closed the door behind her, nostalgia washed over her with the pervasive scent of coffee. What would the next owners do with this place?

Don't go there. Don't think about it.

She grabbed the bucket, filled the pail and started cleaning up. Her ankle still bothered her but she pushed on through the pain welcoming its distraction.

She thought the work would help keep her thoughts at bay, but, as was usual, her mind kept circling back to her conversation with Luke.

Had she been too hasty? Was she wrong in breaking away from him while her heart was supposedly still whole?

And how would you have felt if you carried on just a little longer? And he found out just a little more about you?

He might have been able to stand it.

Janie's second thoughts circled back on themselves, counterpointed by Luke's accusation as she walked out of the bank.

"You're scared of happiness."

She wasn't. She wanted happiness as much as the next divorced/widowed single mother of three children did. She wanted to have a whole and fulfilled life.

But she had found out the hard way that happiness was fleeting and ephemeral. That people's love can turn on a dime to anger and disillusionment when the truth comes out.

She didn't want to see that in Luke's eyes. She preferred to stay the woman who turned him down because of some flaw she saw in him, rather than the other way around. It was easier to let him keep his dream of Janie's perfect family than to lay bare the realities she struggled with every day.

She forced her thoughts back to the job at hand as she packed the leftover coffee and a few personal items back to her car.

She had to go home and change and get ready for her interview.

Two hours and two Advil later, she pulled up in front of her house.

She was done. She had done what she could. The interview at the Inn went well. Tomorrow she had one scheduled at the bank. Though she was fairly sure she'd make more as a waitress, the hours were not conducive to maintaining a healthy family life.

All she needed now was a few precious moments alone. A few moments to gather her thoughts. To let the fact of losing her business sink in before she picked up her children. She needed a break from the ever-present bickering that had entered her family ever since she had walked away from Luke.

As she parked in front of her house, her eyes, as was her usual habit now, turned to Luke's house.

And the For Sale sign on the lawn.

She felt a cold space in the center of her heart as she walked to her house and let herself in.

It was over. Luke hadn't bought the house from his partner after all. They were sticking to their original plan.

For a few days she had harbored the secret hope, a slender wisp of expectation, that he might come over. Might once again cross the boundary she had placed between them.

But he stayed on his side of the fence and she stayed on hers, waiting for the day that never came.

Ignoring her tired feet and aching head, she rinsed the breakfast dishes she hadn't had time to clean in the morning and loaded them in the dishwasher.

The house seemed especially empty as she worked her way through the house from room to room, bottom to top. She felt as if she had been storing up exhaustion for weeks but didn't dare give in. She was on her own. She had to keep going, power through this.

She was just about to turn on the vacuum cleaner when the phone rang. Janie glanced at the clock. How did the time manage to fly by so quickly? It was already quarter to nine. She was going to be late picking up her kids.

She dropped the plug and picked up the phone, ready to make her apologies to her mother.

"Janie. Do you have Serena Allyson's phone number? That girl that Suzie was going to after school? There are about four Allysons in the directory and I can't remember which one Suzie was going to."

Janie frowned. "Why do you need it?"

"She's not home yet."

A flutter of worry started up in Janie's midsection.

"Did she say anything to you?" Tilly said.

"No, but I did say she could stay a bit longer."

"I hope she's not gotten into trouble."

So did Janie. "I'll phone around. See what I can find out."

"You find her, okay?" As Tilly spoke, Janie heard an unfamiliar trembling in her mother's voice, which immediately triggered mother-worry.

Where would Suzie be? she thought as she pulled out her phone book. On impulse, she glanced at the calendar. Nothing was written on today's date, a surprise in itself. Then she remembered Suzie's nagging when she'd dropped Suzie off.

That little stinker, she thought, snatching the phone off the cradle. She punched in Serena's number and paced the kitchen as she waited for someone to pick up.

Serena's parents were home, and they were watching a movie with the family. How nice, Janie thought as she waited for Serena to come to the phone. How very unlike her own messy family life right now.

"Hey, Serena, have you seen Suzie anytime today? She said she was working on your science fair project," Janie asked, keeping her voice light and cheery, trying to sound as if she wasn't sick with worry about where her daughter might be and what she might be doing.

"I heard her say something about going to Riley Watson's place with Tabitha after we were done."

"Who is Riley Watson?"

Serena lowered her voice. "He's in high school, and I think he's having a party tonight."

The party Suzie had been nagging her about for the past month.

"Do you know where he lives?"

"Up on the hill. In those fancy houses. That's all I know."

That narrowed it down to about thirty or forty places, Janie thought, seeing herself cruising through the neighborhood looking for a potential party.

"Thanks, Serena. That helps a bit."

"Hey, I told her not to go. But she really wanted to find out for herself what a high school party is like."

"And that she will," Janie said.

"I'll be praying for you and her," Serena said just before Janie said goodbye.

Of course you will be, Janie thought. You have wonderful parents who do all the right things. A father and a mother who love you and want you and who don't resent you and a mother who had probably never once harbored ideas of giving you up for adoption, or worse, sweeping you from her life.

And, once again, the guilt rose up and accused her. It was

her own fault, she thought as she ran down the hallway to the front door. She was no different than Luke's mother.

At all.

Chapter Seventeen

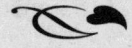

"Near as I figure, you should be able to clear your expenses and make a reasonable profit with this offer."

Luke switched the cell phone to his other ear as he shifted down. "Sounds good enough for me. I just want to move it."

"If you weren't in a rush—"

"But I am. So please, let's get together with these people, and we can sign something."

"Okay. If that's how you want to do it. Once again, I apologize for phoning you so late, but you did tell me you wanted to hear the second I had a potential buyer."

"Don't worry about the hour." Ten o'clock on a Friday night and he was fielding phone calls from a real estate agent. What a great life he had. "I'll be available first thing Monday morning."

"And the building? The tenant has moved out—"

The tenant being Janie. He resented the sense of helpless yearning that washed over him at the thought that she had to do this all alone.

It was what she wanted, he reminded himself. She doesn't want you in her and her kids' life. Let it go.

"Leave that for now. I'll try to off-load it in a couple of weeks." Once he got the house sold and he had hit the no-turning-back point, Riverbend and all the hopes and dreams he had pinned to it were gone.

Luke put up with another apology, a few more pleasantries then said goodbye, but as he flipped his cell phone shut, he felt a lingering regret, a feeling that maybe he should heed the man's advice and wait.

For what? It had been over two weeks since Janie had walked out of his house, her words still shaming and condemning him.

She had the perfect life and there was no room in it for imperfect him.

He glanced down at his speedometer and pulled his foot back. A speeding ticket would be just the thing to top off an already stellar week.

His cell phone rang again, and he glanced at the call display. Not a number he recognized.

"Hey. Luke speaking."

"Luke. Is that you?"

"Suzie?" He hardly recognized the teary voice. "What's wrong? Are you okay? Is it your mom?" His heart thudded in his chest. He knew he should have checked on her once in awhile.

"Not my mom. Luke, can you help me?"

"Yeah. Of course. What's wrong?"

"Can you come get me? I'm at a party and, well…" Her voice faltered, and in the background, he could hear laughing and then the distinctive sound of glass breaking.

"Where are you?"

She gave him an address, which meant nothing. "Just give me directions from the bridge," he said. "Hopefully I can figure it out from there."

"Keep going past Main Street, past the feed mill, across a ravine, then up the hill a bunch. There are some new houses. That's where I am."

He pushed his foot down on the gas, hoping no Mounties were cruising around here. From the sound of the party, they might even be there already.

"I'll pick you up at the front of the house."

The only reply he got was a sniff.

"Suzie. Did you hear me?"

"Can you hurry up?" The plaintive note in her voice caught him in his solar plexus.

He swung around a slow-moving car, passed a truck pulling a stock trailer and ignored the honking horn of a truck that he cut off.

A few minutes later he headed up the hill toward the houses he presumed were the ones Suzie meant.

He swung up the first street, but things looked very suburban and peaceful. Ditto the next street. On the third, he hit pay dirt. Cars and trucks lined the street, and one house was ablaze with light. Even from inside his truck he could hear the music. But no police. Yet.

He parked at the end of the street, got out of the truck and surveyed his surroundings. No sense in jumping directly into a party full of teenage boys and rampant egos greased with liquor.

But the urgency in Suzie's voice hurried his steps.

A girl stood at the end of the sidewalk, staring at the house, as if trying to make up her mind if she should go in or not.

Suzie?

No. This was an older person—probably another parent. As Luke came closer, he realized he was right.

Then his heart started up again. The parent was Suzie's mother.

Janie. He swallowed down the knot of expectation her presence caused. So quickly, he thought. So easily she could do that to him.

He didn't need to be here. She could take care of this himself, but he couldn't stop, drawn to this woman like a moth to a flame.

"Hey, Janie," he said, raising his voice above the music pounding from inside the house.

She spun around, her hand on her chest, her face lit up by the lights blazing from the house. "Luke. What are you doing here?"

"Suzie called me." Because he had to yell, he was sure she couldn't hear the way his pounding heart made his voice tremble.

"Why did she call you? What was she thinking?"

"I don't know."

"It's okay. You can go. I've got this under control."

Of course she did. His emotions morphed into anger, and all the frustration and hurt he'd been pushing down spilled out as his words exploded into the night. "Right. Like you've got everything else in your precious life under control." He didn't mean to sound so harsh, but spending two weeks away from her had been an exercise in frustration. Especially when, the entire time, she was often no more than forty feet away.

Many times he'd had to stop himself from wanting to go over to replace that loose faucet in the kitchen that she said she was going to buy. Fix the shingles on the roof. Paint that peeling trim.

But she would never ask.

"I don't need your help," she said. "My family doesn't need your help."

"Oh, yeah? Then why did Suzie call me and not you?"

The hurt on her face almost made him regret his anger. Almost. She was so independent. So incredibly, stubbornly independent.

"I didn't have to come here, but I did because I care about Suzie and I care about you. I want to help you and have wanted to help you ever since I first saw you. And not because I feel sorry for you or see you as a charity case. It's because I care. And when you care about someone, you want to make their life easier. You want to do things for them. And you shouldn't let their precious pride get in the way like I have with you." The relentless onslaught of words spilling out of his mouth caught him by surprise. He stopped right there and took a breath to calm himself.

Janie kept her eyes straight ahead. He had no idea what was going on behind that tight expression or those narrowed blue eyes. He'd made a special trip to help out her daughter, and this was the thanks he got?

In the meantime, Suzie was inside and she needed help.

A crowd of kids spilled onto the front lawn, backlit by the lights of the house, laughing and dancing in time to the music pouring out the front door.

He started up the walk, but Janie caught him by the sleeve, stopping him. "Why are you getting involved? This isn't your problem."

"Who says?" He was still angry with her, but as she glanced from the noisy house to him, the worry on her face eased his frustration.

"I…I don't want you to see this," she said.

Luke had to strain to hear her.

"See what?"

"The mess. My daughter, who you think is so perfect, messing up. Me, a mother, messing up."

"How is this you messing up?"

"You wouldn't understand."

His anger spilled out again.

"You think I wouldn't understand. You don't want me to understand. You want to keep yourself all safe and contained," he said. "You want to keep everything in your life to yourself and make sure that no one steps over that boundary you defend."

Stop, now. She doesn't need this lecture. Not coming from someone like you. And Suzie is in that house and needs your help.

But he was angry, frustrated and had nothing to lose.

Because when Janie had walked out of his house, he'd felt as if he had lost everything he had wanted in his life.

"It's not that easy, Luke. And you're not that uncomplicated yourself," she shot back, her eyes narrowing. "You've got your own stuff that you're not letting people see, so don't stand there and accuse me of keeping you at arm's length. Because that's exactly what you have done to me."

Luke was taken aback at her anger. And then, curiously, encouraged by it. If she didn't care, she wouldn't be angry.

"Okay. I've kept things from you. I was wrong. But I had my reasons."

"Well, so do I."

"Then maybe we should sit down and talk about these reasons. And maybe we should go get your daughter so we can go home and do exactly that."

"I'm scared to go inside."

He gave her a gentle smile, his anger fading in the face of her honesty. "You're not a lousy mother. Now I'm going to get Suzie." Luke turned to Janie. "You may as well stay out here, unless you want to come inside with me."

"I'll stay here."

Luke hadn't imagined the relief on her face; he heard it clearly in her voice.

Luke nodded, then, unable to leave her standing there,

alone and afraid, he caught her by the shoulder and squeezed. "I'll find her, okay?"

"Please do." Janie gave him a tremulous smile, but he could see the glint of tears in her eyes. "And thanks."

He turned back to the house. *Please, Lord, help me not to hit anyone who tries to stop me,* he prayed as he strode up the walk.

The noise inside was, if possible, even louder than outside.

A young couple standing in the doorway gave him a puzzled look as he sauntered past them. A quick scan of the foyer yielded a group of girls squealing at something a boy above them on the stairs was yelling down.

He hesitated a moment, then made a guess and turned right. Away from the noise of the stereo.

"Hey, whaddaya doin' here?" A young man with a buzz cut stepped in front of Luke, his muscle-bound arms crossed over his chest.

"I came to pick up a girl."

Mr. Buzz Cut laughed and punched him on the shoulder. "Good luck with that," he said, obviously misinterpreting Luke's intent.

Luke wanted to punch him back, but not in a friendly way. Then he saw Suzie. She sat on the floor, by the French doors, a boy about five years older than her sitting beside her. She looked terrified.

"Suzie?" he called out. She jumped to her feet and came running toward him. Luke hardly recognized Janie's daughter, overly made up with skintight jeans and cropped T-shirt.

"Can we go now?" she cried, grabbing him by the arm.

The boy who sat with her lurched to his feet and walked unsteadily over. "Hey. She was with me."

"Not anymore," Luke said, staring down at the kid.

The boy frowned. "You think you're tough?"

Luke enunciated each word slowly and carefully. "Don't even bother."

The boy took a step back, his hands up. "Sorry."

Luke waited a moment, driving home his point. Then he took Suzie by one slender arm and marched her to the door.

She seemed okay. That much he had figured out. No one had stopped them or challenged him. They were in the clear.

Now his anger was directed at the young girl. He yanked open the front door and strode with her down the sidewalk to where Janie waited.

"You took my mom along?" Suzie wailed, pulling back.

"She came here on her own."

Janie stayed at the end of the sidewalk until they stopped in front of her.

"Are you okay, Suzie?" she asked, reaching out to her daughter.

Suzie didn't even look at her.

"I'll take her home," Luke said.

To his surprise, Janie nodded, pulling her arm back.

"I'll meet you back at the house," he said, taking a chance when he reached out and cupped her cheek.

She caught his hand and pressed it between her cheek and her hand, then let go, turned and walked across the street to her car.

Luke waited until she left, and then he brought Suzie to his truck and helped her inside. As he got in, he looked over at the young girl, crouched against the door.

Streaks of black marred her innocent cheeks, and her blue eyes were like large circles of purple and pink. She sniffed and wiped the palm of her hand over her face, smearing the makeup even further.

"Buckle up, missy," he said as he reversed into a neighbor's driveway, slammed the truck into gear and sped down the street.

"You sound mad," she sniffed as he heard the snick of her buckle going into the clasp.

"I'm furious, actually." He thought of Janie standing at the end of the sidewalk, afraid to go inside the house and get her own daughter. Afraid to let him go in and see her daughter.

"What were you thinking?" he asked, shooting the question across the cab. "No. Wait. That's a dumb question. You weren't thinking, were you? You had some crazy idea that going to a party with a bunch of high school kids was going to be just the highlight of your year. Something you could brag to all your friends about. Well, it looks like you had a blast, didn't you?"

"Why are you so mad at me? I thought you would help me."

"I did." Luke spun the truck around a corner and then forced himself to slow down. "I got you out of that party and away from trouble. And I kept your mother from having to go in and get you. Do you have any idea of how worried you must have made her?"

"I'm sorry," she said in a small, contrite voice.

Luke pressed his lips together, biting off his next comment. In spite of his tough talk to Janie, he didn't have any right to be blasting away at Suzie. As a mother, that was her job.

They drove the rest of the way home in silence. By the time he parked by Janie's car in front of the house, he felt calmer.

He followed her up the sidewalk to the house where Janie waited.

"Oh, Suzie. Are you okay?" Janie caught her daughter by the arms, then enveloped her in a hug. "I was so worried."

"I'm sorry, Mom," Suzie said, clinging to her mother. "I'm sorry I made you worry."

"You're okay?" Janie pulled back, her hands fluttering over her daughter's face.

Suzie nodded.

"I'm so proud of you that you called Luke. That was exactly the right thing to do."

What was this all about? Luke glanced from Suzie to Janie, trying to figure out why Janie wasn't blasting her even harder than he had.

"Can I have some leftover pizza?" Suzie asked. "I'm hungry."

"I think I have some left."

Luke held up a hand. "Wait a minute, did I miss something here?" Luke's eyes ticked from Janie to Suzie.

"What do you mean?" Janie asked, looking as puzzled as Luke felt.

"I just hauled this girl from a lousy situation that she put herself in. And you're fussing about her missing supper?"

He saw Janie's face grow stiff but he pushed on. "I think she should be grounded so hard that she can't see the sky for a month."

"I hardly think—"

"And I think she should get upstairs right now and wash that gunk off her face." Luke pointed upward, and to his surprise, Suzie meekly pulled away from her mother. "Suzie, get going."

She didn't even give him a second look and ran up the stairs.

Janie watched Suzie go, then turned to him, frowning. "Luke, she's my daughter and I think I know how to deal with this."

"I thought we covered this already."

Janie pulled back, her frown replaced with hurt.

Luke shoved his hand through his hair, frustrated, yet knowing he was right. "I'm sorry, Janie, but you're way too easy on that girl. She needs to be disciplined for what she did tonight, not hugged and kissed and told she's a good girl."

Luke could see Janie's protest rise to her lips, but then she stopped herself. "You're right."

"Of course I am. I may not be a father, but I'd like to think I know a few things."

He wanted to say more, but the ringing of the doorbell broke into the moment, and Janie's mother swept into the house with Autumn and Todd.

Her eyes flicked over him and then landed on her daughter.

"Where is Suzie? Did you find her? Is she all right?"

Tilly peppered Janie with questions as she pulled Autumn's jacket off.

"She's upstairs. Luke brought her home."

"Thank you, Luke. That was much appreciated." Tilly gave him a curt nod, as if dismissing him.

Luke felt suddenly superfluous. "I'll be leaving now," he said to Janie.

Janie glanced from him to his mother.

"We should get these kids in bed, Janie," her mother was saying. "And then we can deal with Suzie."

Luke stepped toward the door when he heard, "Wait a minute."

He turned, and Janie was walking toward him. She glanced back at her mother. "Mom, can you put the kids to bed please?"

Tilly frowned and was about to protest.

"I need to talk to Luke," Janie continued. "And I need to do that without any children around."

"Well, if you think that's what you should be doing," Tilly said, as if she expected Janie to change her mind.

"I do," Janie said as she walked out the door ahead of Luke.

Chapter Eighteen

"It's a nice night. Do you mind if we walk for a bit?" Janie asked, as the door of her house closed behind her.

"Excellent idea."

His deep voice had lowered, and in the gathering dark, Janie felt as if the world had narrowed down to the two of them.

Part of her still felt surprised that she had stood up to her mother, but now she needed to just be with Luke. To gather her thoughts.

She was quiet as they walked down her sidewalk, past the potted plants that were just starting to fill out, then past Luke's house with its single light on upstairs. Cooper, sensing their presence from inside the house, gave a muffled bark.

They moved into a pool of light from a streetlamp, then out. By the time they crossed the street to the next block, she still hadn't said anything, and thankfully Luke seemed content to saunter along in silence while she gathered her thoughts.

"Thanks for going into that party and bringing Suzie home," she said finally, as they crossed the next street.

"You're welcome."

"I'm glad you were there. I'm glad…glad you forced me to allow your help."

"Me, too."

She sighed. "When I got to that house, I wasn't sure what to do. And then, when you came…" She paused, unsure of how to continue, yet, at the same time, sure she wanted him to know how she felt.

"When you came, I felt so relieved. I felt like I wasn't alone."

"I didn't get that impression."

"This isn't easy for me, okay?"

"I'm sorry."

"I know I've always been independent. I've always thought I could solve all my problems on my own. The past few weeks have showed me I can't. And this evening definitely showed me I couldn't. Even though I didn't show it, I was glad for your help."

She drew in a breath of the soft night air. A hint of dampness promised rain.

"But other things were going on when you came. That's why I was so angry. I stood at the end of that sidewalk for about ten minutes," she said, "trying to work up the nerve to go in. I didn't want to see Suzie inside. Didn't want to see her…reliving my life."

"What do you mean?"

"I didn't want to see her make the same mistakes I did. Do the same dumb things. Go to the same dumb parties."

"You? Partying?"

His surprise made her feel worse, but what hurt more was seeing him standing in front of that house, knowing Suzie had called him and not her.

"It was hard enough for me to have to see my daughter mess up. I guess I wasn't crazy about the idea of you seeing it, too."

"Everyone makes mistakes, Janie."

"Yeah, but it was especially difficult after you made me look like such a great mother, such a great person. I felt like the whole mess of my life was laid out for you to see. And I was afraid for you to see even a small part of that."

"What? Why?"

Janie kept her eyes directly ahead, focusing on the sidewalk and the next pool of light.

"I've had a complicated relationship with Suzie ever since I found out I was expecting her. I was eighteen, it was the first year of college and I had just broken up with her father, Owen. When I sat on the edge of the bathtub that night staring at the blue on the strip, my entire life with all its glorious plans made a giant U-turn."

She paused there, her old shame slithering into the moment. "I was young and confused and overwhelmed."

Luke's only reply was to gently squeeze her arm. Janie moved to pull her arm out of his, to give herself some distance from him. She didn't want to feel his reaction to what she had to tell him next.

But he wouldn't let her go.

And in spite of her initial reaction, she was comforted by his support. His strength.

"There's more," she said quietly.

"I can hear it."

She hoped he could. She prayed he could. "When I first found out I was pregnant, I was scared…I wanted to fix this problem…I…"

Could she do this? Could she really lay open her heart?

She looked up at Luke and saw him smiling down at her. Would that smile disappear if she told him?

She had to. He had accused her of being independent and he had been right. She had kept this to herself so long.

She had missed him too much. She knew she wanted him in her life, and she now knew that would mean all of her life. *Please, Lord, help me to say this,* Janie prayed. *I know I should have told someone a long time ago. Forgive me.*

"When I first found out, I wanted to have an abortion. I talked to a woman at a clinic in Edmonton. Tried to figure out how I could get away to get it done." She took a shuddering breath, praying he would understand. "I didn't want my own child."

"But you didn't go through with it." Luke rested his hand on her shoulder, a gentle assurance.

Janie kept her focus on her feet. Step, pause, step, pause. A slow meandering rhythm. "I couldn't make up my mind, and then it was too late. So my next plan was to put her up for adoption. Then my mother found out, and my life took another turn. And, even worse, I resented Suzie for putting me in this mess in the first place. For the longest time I felt, because of her, I ended up a mother, married to a man who never cared for me and never loved me. I have always struggled with how I felt about Suzie. And I guess that's why it seems like I treat her differently. Maybe not always wisely, but I feel like I have so much to make up for."

Step, pause, step, pause. Luke hadn't said anything yet so Janie continued.

"When you asked me why I was defending your mother, I think…I think I was defending myself. When I heard you say that she didn't deserve your love, your respect, I felt as if you were talking about me."

Luke stopped, caught her arm and gently turned her to face him. "No. Janie. Never. My mother made her own mistakes. Different from you."

Janie gave a short laugh at his quick defense of her and looked up at him, holding his steady gaze. "I was single, pregnant and confused. I didn't want my own daughter. Doesn't sound too different from your mother. When you said you couldn't forgive your mother for that, it was as if I was unforgivable."

Luke slowly shook his head, his fingers coming to rest on her cheek. "So when you heard me say that, you thought I would feel the same way about you."

"I did." She shivered, and Luke rubbed her arms.

"But you provided a home for Suzie and your other kids. You take care of them. You love them. They know they're loved."

"But Suzie…tonight…" Janie pulled her jacket tighter around her, tension holding her captive.

"Tonight is also not unusual. Every kid wants to go to a party when they're teenagers. She just happened to find a way to do it."

"You seem to be willing to sweep away what I've thought, what Suzie has done—"

"I'm not sweeping it away. I'm the one who thought she should be grounded, after all. I'm trying to show you that some of the things you've taken on are normal reactions and actions."

"But it was different for your mother?"

Luke sighed, and she sensed she was treading, once again, on shaky ground.

"My mother's problems are more complicated…" He paused there, as if thinking. "But I went to see her the other night. After you told me that you couldn't be with me. Something you said made me realize that maybe she was coming between us. Maybe I needed to find some kind of peace with her in order to move on. In order to build some kind of life with you."

Janie felt hope surge in her chest, but she let the moment hang.

"She's made a lot of mistakes, but she's human. And I knew

that as long as I was angry with her and hurt by her, I wasn't going to be able to move on in my own life. In my own faith. I had felt distant from God for some time, now I think it was because of how I felt toward my mother. And especially now that I know that you felt the same about Suzie…" Luke turned to her. "We still have a long way to go, my mother and I, but we're starting. I read a piece in the Bible about forgiving as Christ has forgiven us. I'd like to think that, with God's help, I'm getting there. I'd also like to think that you could help me."

Janie took a chance herself, reached up and cupped his face in her hand. "I want to. I need to. Because if you can forgive your mother, then I can feel that Suzie will, in time, forgive me."

"She will. And she'll appreciate all that you've done in the meantime. And if she doesn't, I will remind her."

Janie rested in his embrace, thankful for his support. His care.

She leaned back and looked up into his dark, intense gaze. "I missed you."

"I missed you, too. And I don't want to miss you anymore."

He smiled down at her, then bending over, he kissed her. His mouth was warm and gentle, and Janie melted into his embrace.

When he pulled away, her heart was beating quickly, her cheeks flushed and she felt as if her feet didn't touch the ground.

He smiled down at her, then slowly drew in a breath. "I love you, Janie."

His simple declaration surrounded her. Filled the empty places. "I love you, too." Janie stroked his cheek, resting her fingertips on his mouth. "And I'm glad you came into my life. You've taught me a lot. About letting people help. About not trying to do everything myself. And I think I'll need your help. For a long time."

Luke rested his forehead against hers, and the sigh he released seemed to embody her feelings as well.

"That sounds like a proposal."

"Well, I think that's your job."

"I would hope so."

She stood on tiptoe and brushed a kiss over his lips. He caught her close and deepened the kiss full of promises and hope.

"So, I suppose we should go back to the house. The kids will be wondering what is going on."

"And what do we tell them?" Luke asked, his voice holding a gentle intimacy as they turned around. "That for better or for worse—"

"For richer or for poorer," Janie added her voice to the quiet vow.

"I'm looking forward to telling them."

"And of course, after that, we'll have to tell my mom and dad and Dodie. Aunt Dot and Uncle Morris, Ethan and Hannah and Francine. Uncle Fred and Sarah and Logan." She gave him a rueful smile. "You're not just getting me and the kids, you know. You're getting a clan."

"I've never had a big family."

Janie hesitated, then plunged in. "And your mother. She'll need to know."

Luke glanced down at her, but he was still smiling. "Of course." He brushed his lips over hers, as if drawing from her. "I'd like you to come with me. I'd like her to formally meet you."

"Maybe we could take the kids along. Go all together."

"Together. I like the sound of that."

"And we can't forget Cooper."

"Especially Cooper. He does have a stake in the relationship," Luke said with a laugh. "After all, if it wasn't for him…"

"I'd still have some nice petunias."

Luke laughed and gave her another hug.

"And the house?" Janie asked. "Are you still selling it?"

"I don't know. I'm kind of attached to it, though I did buy it with my partner to flip it. I might have to buy him out, after all."

"You know, if you're interested, I know of another place you could pick up on the cheap that could use some work," Janie said, letting a coy note enter her voice.

"I don't know. I have a bunch of money tied up in a building downtown. Used to have a coffee shop in it?"

Janie frowned, trying to gather what he said. "You bought the building?"

"I had plans. Lots of plans. Something about a bookstore run in conjunction with a coffee shop…" He let the sentence, rife with promises and expectation, drift into the night.

Janie laughed. "So you're the mystery buyer."

He nodded.

"That's unexpected."

"It's the way I operate."

Janie held his gaze as her mind flipped back to the first time she saw him. How she resented his intrusion in her life. His and Cooper's.

And now she stood in the circle of his arms, the promise of a future shimmering around them both.

A family. For both of them.

Epilogue

Two months later

"Luke. Can you put this on the table?" Janie took a platter of ham from the oven and set it on the island between the kitchen and the dining room. She nudged Cooper aside and walked to the refrigerator to get the sauce she'd made just this afternoon.

Luke frowned, and then his eyes met hers across the kitchen and he grinned. "Sorry, I was just helping Todd with the two-headed Hydra."

"How supportive of you," she said smiling at her husband.

Luke frowned as he reached for the platter. "I thought Suzie was helping you?"

"She's getting a bowl from the other house."

Luke set the platter on a table that already held three salads, a bowl of buns, gravy and sour cream. "You realize you won't have room here for the potatoes."

The ringing of the doorbell sent Cooper scurrying across the tile floor.

"Cooper, down." Luke and Janie cried out in unison.

Cooper skidded to a halt before he got to the wood floor of the hallway, then turned to look at Luke and Janie as if checking to see if they were indeed serious.

"Hello, the house," Dodie called out from the front door. "We're here."

Dodie was shrugging off her coat, walking toward the closet in the hallway as her parents stepped into the house. Her mother carried a bouquet of flowers, her father a jug of sweet cider.

"Come on in," Janie said, shivering as the cool fall air followed her parents inside.

Her mother was looking around the house, her eyes missing nothing. Janie resisted the urge to straighten the rug Cooper had been lying on moments before and to pick up the toys Autumn had dropped before she went upstairs to change.

"Hello, hello," her mother said, handing Janie the flowers. She leaned forward and kissed her daughter. Then, as she stepped back, reached out and straightened Janie's collar. "The house looks lovely. Are you all moved in?"

"I'm sure it will take a couple of weeks yet, but we're getting there."

"Have you sold the other place yet?" her father asked as he looked around the entrance as well.

"Luke is going to fix it up first."

"In all his spare time?" Dan Westerveld asked, pushing open the doors leading to the living room.

"The shop is going pretty good. Right, Dodie?" Janie asked, staying in the front entrance with her sister.

"Gangbusters," Dodie said as she bent over to fondle Cooper's ears. "Though I don't know how impressed Luke is with the knitting concept I want to introduce to that empty corner of the bookstore."

"You still campaigning for your knitting corner?" Luke asked as he met his in-laws coming through the door from the living room into the dining area. "Hello, Tilly. Dan."

"I've got the bowl," Suzie announced as she stepped into the kitchen from the back door.

"Here I am," Autumn announced, pushing Cooper aside as she came down the stairs.

The family converged on the dining room. As Janie put the flowers in water, she directed Suzie, who was mashing the potatoes.

The talk circled from the house, to the changing cost of real estate, to the business Luke and Janie had set up in the building Luke had purchased.

"I think we can eat," she said as Suzie put the steaming bowl mounded with yellow potatoes on the table.

Luke frowned at the place settings as everyone found a chair and sat down. "You put out one too many," he said, just as the doorbell rang again.

Relief surged through Janie. "Just sit down. I'm expecting someone else."

She ignored Luke's frown as she hurried down the hall, hoping, praying. Then she opened the door and there stood Luke's mother.

She held a fruit platter and wore beige slacks, a leather jacket and a tentative smile.

"Am I too late?" she asked.

Janie glanced over her shoulder as Luke joined them in the front hall. His frown slowly shifted, and Janie saw in his eyes a flash of hope.

"You're right on time, Lillian," Janie said, stepping aside to let Luke's mother in. "Suzie, can you take the fruit platter from Ms. Harris and put it on the island?"

"Why can't Todd do it?" she complained.

"Because you're my slave," Janie said with a wink.

Suzie just rolled her eyes but thankfully did as she was told.

"Thanks for having me," Lillian said, her smile tentative.

Luke's arm tightened around Janie's shoulder. "Thanks for coming, Mom."

"So, shall we eat?" Janie asked. "I'm sure everyone's hungry. Suzie, can you show Lillian where she'll be sitting?"

Suzie nodded, then turned and led the way into the dining area. Janie was about to follow when Luke pulled her back. He turned her to face him, his expression bemused. "You're an amazing woman, Janie Harris. Have I ever told you that?"

"Not for the last few minutes," Janie returned with a teasing smile.

"I'm losing my touch." He stroked her face, cupped her cheek and brushed a lingering kiss over her lips. "Well, you are. And God has blessed me beyond blessings."

"And me, Luke," Janie said, returning his kiss.

"Can we eat?" Autumn called out. "Cooper is hungry."

"We'd better go," Janie said. "Don't want to keep our family waiting."

"Our family." Luke smiled. "I like the sound of that."

* * * * *

Dear Reader,

This story came to me as I was watching my daughter's dog, also a golden Lab, also a Cooper, running around the yard. He was so full of life and energy, most of it uncontrolled at the time. So I wondered what would happen if a dog like that were to burst into the lives of a woman and her family. A woman who wanted—needed—control.

A woman like Janie Corbett.

The dog would, of course, need an owner who felt adrift. Enter Luke with his desire for family and connection. And because he lived next door…

This is a theme that comes up frequently in my books and is, in fact, the theme of my Web site—Coming Home to Family and Faith. I believe we are all looking for a connection of one sort or another. We find it in family, community. We find it in our pets.

But I pray that you may find your strongest connection in the Lord, who is constantly seeking us and waiting for us to find Him.

If you want to find out more about me and my other Love Inspired books, stop by my Web site:

www.carolyneaarsen.com.

Carolyne Aarsen

QUESTIONS FOR DISCUSSION

1. What do you think is the theme of this book?

2. Which character did you sympathize with most, and why?

3. Luke was seeking family. Why do you think he didn't bother to look to his mother for what he needed?

4. Why do you think Luke kept avoiding his mother? Was he justified in doing so?

5. Why do you think Janie kept Luke at arm's length?

6. Who was Janie protecting more, herself or her children?

7. How did this book make you look at the people in your own life?

8. Has the author of this book portrayed faith realistically? Why or why not?

9. How are pets important in our lives?

10. Do you think our society places too much importance on pets? Why or why not?

11. Luke had to learn to forgive his mother. Is there someone in your life you are struggling to forgive?

12. How was Luke's attitude toward his mother hampering his faith life? Was Janie right to challenge him?

13. When do we decide that we have forgiven enough? Is there such a time?

Love Inspired
HISTORICAL

*Powerful, engaging stories of romance, adventure
and faith set in the past—when things were simpler
and faith played a major role in everyday lives.*

Turn the page for a sneak preview of
THE MAVERICK PREACHER
by
Victoria Bylin

*Love Inspired Historical—love and
faith throughout the ages*

Mr. Blue looked into her eyes with silent understanding and she wondered if he, too, had a struggled with God's ways. The slash of his brow looked tight with worry, and his whiskers were too stubbly to be permanent. Adie thought about his shaving tools and wondered when he'd used them last. Her new boarder would clean up well on the outside, but his heart remained a mystery. She needed to keep it that way. The less she knew about him, the better.

"Good night," she said. "Bessie will check you in the morning."

"Before you go, I've been wondering…"

"About what?"

"The baby… Who's the mother?"

Adie raised her chin. "I am."

Earlier he'd called her "Miss Clarke" and she hadn't corrected him. The flash in his eyes told her that he'd assumed she'd given birth out of wedlock. Adie resented being judged, but she counted it as the price of protecting Stephen. If Mr. Blue chose to condemn her, so be it. She'd done nothing for which to be ashamed. With their gazes locked, she waited for the criticism that didn't come.

Instead he laced his fingers on top of the Bible. "Children are a gift, all of them."

"I think so, too."

He lightened his tone. "A boy or a girl?"

"A boy."

The man smiled. "He sure can cry. How old is he?"

Adie didn't like the questions at all, but she took pride in her son. "He's three months old." She didn't mention that he'd been born six weeks early. "I hope the crying doesn't disturb you."

"I don't care if it does."

He sounded defiant. She didn't understand. "Most men would be annoyed."

"The crying's better than silence…. I know."

Adie didn't want to care about this man, but her heart fluttered against her ribs. What did Joshua Blue know of babies and silence? Had he lost a wife? A child of his own? She wanted to express sympathy but couldn't. If she pried into his life, he'd pry into hers. He'd ask questions and she'd have to hide the truth. *Stephen was born too soon and his mother died. He barely survived. I welcome his cries, every one of them. They mean he's alive.*

With a lump in her throat, she turned to leave. "Good night, Mr. Blue."

"Good night."

A thought struck her and she turned back to his room. "I supposed I should call you Reverend."

He grimaced. "I'd prefer Josh."

* * * * *

*Don't miss this deeply moving Love Inspired Historical
story about a man of God who's lost his way
and the woman who helps him rediscover
his faith—and his heart.
THE MAVERICK PREACHER
by Victoria Bylin
available February 2009.*

*And also look for
THE MARSHAL TAKES A BRIDE
by Renee Ryan,
in which a lawman meets his match in a
feisty schoolteacher with marriage on her mind.*

Love Inspired.
HISTORICAL
INSPIRATIONAL HISTORICAL ROMANCE

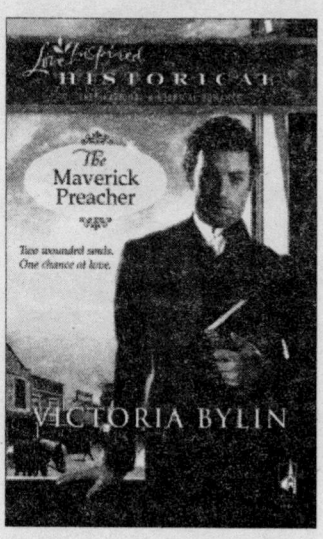

Adelaide Clark has worked hard to raise her young son on her own, and Boston minister Joshua Blue isn't going to break up her home. As she grows to trust Joshua, Adie sees he's only come to make amends for his past. Yet Joshua's love sparks a hope for the future that Adie thought was long dead—a future with a husband by her side.

Look for

The Maverick Preacher
by
VICTORIA BYLIN

Available February 2009 wherever books are sold.

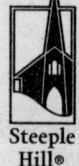

Steeple Hill®

www.SteepleHill.com

Love Inspired

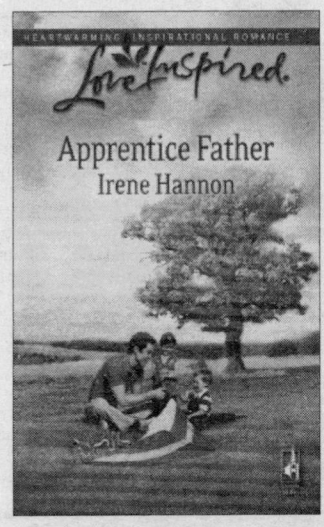

With an orphaned niece and nephew depending on him, commitment-shy Clay Adams calls upon nanny Cate Shepard to save them all. With God's help, Cate's kind, nurturing ways may be able to ease the children into their new lives. And her love could give lone-wolf Clay the forever family he deserves.

Look for

Apprentice Father
by
Irene Hannon

*Available February 2009
wherever books are sold.*

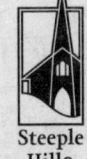

Steeple Hill®

REQUEST YOUR FREE BOOKS!

2 FREE INSPIRATIONAL NOVELS PLUS 2 FREE MYSTERY GIFTS

Love Inspired®

YES! Please send me 2 FREE Love Inspired® novels and my 2 FREE mystery gifts (gifts are worth about $10). After receiving them, if I don't wish to receive any more books, I can return the shipping statement marked "cancel". If I don't cancel, I will receive 4 brand-new novels every month and be billed just $4.24 per book in the U.S. or $4.74 per book in Canada, plus 25¢ shipping and handling per book and applicable taxes, if any*. That's a savings of over 20% off the cover price! I understand that accepting the 2 free books and gifts places me under no obligation to buy anything. I can always return a shipment and cancel at any time. Even if I never buy another book, the two free books and gifts are mine to keep forever.

113 IDN ERXA 313 IDN ERWX

Name	(PLEASE PRINT)	
Address		Apt. #
City	State/Prov.	Zip/Postal Code

Signature (if under 18, a parent or guardian must sign)

Order online at www.LoveInspiredBooks.com

Or mail to Steeple Hill Reader Service:

IN U.S.A.: P.O. Box 1867, Buffalo, NY 14240-1867
IN CANADA: P.O. Box 609, Fort Erie, Ontario L2A 5X3

Not valid to current subscribers of Love Inspired books.

**Want to try two free books from another series?
Call 1-800-873-8635 or visit www.morefreebooks.com**

* Terms and prices subject to change without notice. N.Y. residents add applicable sales tax. Canadian residents will be charged applicable provincial taxes and GST. Offer not valid in Quebec. This offer is limited to one order per household. All orders subject to approval. Credit or debit balances in a customer's account(s) may be offset by any other outstanding balance owed by or to the customer. Please allow 4 to 6 weeks for delivery. Offer available while quantities last.

Your Privacy: Steeple Hill Books is committed to protecting your privacy. Our Privacy Policy is available online at www.SteepleHill.com or upon request from the Reader Service. From time to time we make our lists of customers available to reputable third parties who may have a product or service of interest to you. If you would prefer we not share your name and address, please check here. ☐

LIREG08R

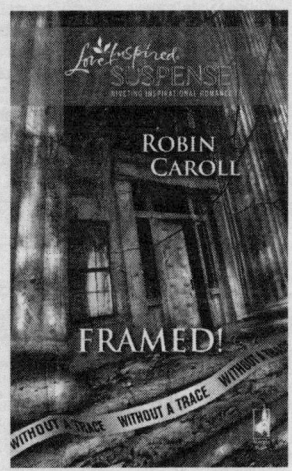

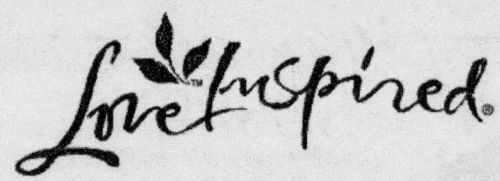

TITLES AVAILABLE NEXT MONTH

Don't miss these four stories on sale January 27, 2009.

APPRENTICE FATHER by Irene Hannon
With an orphaned niece and nephew depending on him, commitment-shy Clay Adams calls upon nanny Cate Shepard to save them all. With God's help and her kind, nurturing ways, Cate may be able to ease the children into their new life. And her love could give lone-wolf Clay the forever family he deserves.

THEIR SMALL-TOWN LOVE by Arlene James
Eden, OK

A high school reunion means a trip home for new Christian Ivy Villard…to mend some fences. Past mistakes await her in tiny Eden, Oklahoma—like her former high school sweetheart, Ryan Jeffords. Yet a second chance at love is waiting for them, if they're brave enough to take it.

A COWBOY'S HEART by Brenda Minton
A lot of folks depend on ex-rodeo star Clint Cameron, including his twin four-year-old nephews. So why can't his stubborn neighbor, Willow Michaels, accept a little help with her bull-raising business? Clint's got a lot more than advice to offer Willow, if only she'd look deep in his faithful, loving heart.

BLUEGRASS COURTSHIP by Allie Pleiter
Kentucky Corners

Rebuilding the church's storm-damaged preschool is easy for the celebrity host of TV's *Missionnovation*, Drew Downing. Rebuilding lovely hardware store owner Janet Bishop's faith in God and love may be a bit more challenging. But Drew is just the man for the job.

LICNMBPA0109